✝Church
✝Architecture

James F. White and Susan J. White

OSL Publications
Akron, Ohio

Church Architecture
Building and Renovating for Christian Worship

New Edition - July 1998
Second Printing - October 1998

ISBN 1-878009-34-6

This book is printed on acid-free paper that meets the
American National Standards Institute Z39.48 Standard

Produced and manufactured in the United States of America by
OSL Publications
The publishing ministry of the Order of Saint Luke
P.O. Box 22279
Akron, OH 44302-0079

http://www.Saint-Luke.org

The Order of Saint Luke is a Religious Order dedicated to sacramental and liturgical scholarship, education and practice. The purpose of the publishing ministry is to put into the hands of students and practitioners resources which have theological, historical, ecumenical and practical integrity.

CONTENTS

For
Todd
and
Martin

The Authors

James F. White is Professor of Liturgical Studies at the University of Notre Dame in South Bend, Indiana. Prior to his current appointment, he taught for 22 years at Perkins School of Theology, Southern Methodist University at Dallas, Texas. His most recent book is *Christian Worship in North America* (Collegeville: Liturgical Press, 1997). Among the 17 books he has authored are included *Roman Catholic Worship* (1995), *Protestant Worship* (1989), *Introduction to Christian Worship* (1990), and *Sacraments as God's Self-Giving* (1983). The year 1998-99 marks his fortieth year in teaching.

Susan J. White is Harold and Alberta Lunger Professor of Spiritual Resources and Disciplines at Brite Divinity School, Texas Christian University in Fort Worth, Texas. Formerly, she taught worship and preaching in the Cambridge Theological Federation and the Faculty of Divinity, Cambridge University in Cambridge, England. She is a lay member of the British Methodist Conference. Her most recent book is *Groundwork of Christian Worship* (London: Epworth Press, 1997).

ONE

A PLACE FOR THE COMMUNITY OF FAITH

Architecture is the organization of space, and church architecture is the organization of space for worship. The architect who helps a community organize space for worship must receive thorough information about what the community does in its worship. Thus we always begin a discussion of church architecture with questions about the intended function of this space: What do we do here?

The relation of architecture to worship is a complex one. Church architecture reflects both the way Christians worship and the way the building shapes worship — or, not uncommonly, misshapes it. As our practices and concepts of worship change, major changes in the building are often necessary. Although we are not quite so pessimistic as to think the building will always prevail, certainly it may be a major obstacle to what the community intends in its worship. At the same time a well-designed building can be a great asset in enabling the community to worship as it desires. Without buildings, we would worship with difficulty; with some, we still worship with difficulty.

Worship, then, is primary in any discussion of church architecture. Every church building should be judged in terms of how well it serves the worshiping community of faith. *The primary symbol of Christian worship is always the community itself, assembled in Christ's name.* His presence is known afresh in each gathering as the community comes together again and again to form the body of Christ. A religion of the incarnation is not confined to past history but to a Christ whose presence is experienced in the life

1

together of the community he established. "Now you are Christ's body," Paul writes, and for this reason the community is the primary symbol of Christ's presence in our midst.

Architecturally, this means that the focus of a Christian church is always on the inside where people gather, not on the outside, as in a pagan temple built as a monument to a god, where the people are excluded from the interior. Christians do not build memorials to an absent god, but places where God and people meet. The facades of many great churches were left unfinished for centuries; the outside really did not matter as long as the community could use the interior.

Several characteristics of such priorities should be mentioned. Our times have recognized the quality of *hospitality* as being important to church buildings. A church must be inviting in order to welcome all comers and make them feel at home. We are more likely to think of hospitality in terms of private homes, yet many qualities of domestic architecture are now recognized as desirable in churches, too. It is no accident that in missionary situations, the church has always felt comfortable meeting in private residences, whether in first-century Rome or twentieth-century Africa. Every church building functions in the process of evangelization, either by making people feel welcome or by repelling them. It is never neutral territory. The essence of hospitality is to bring people together so they want to meet, know each other, and act together with a common purpose.

Many factors enter into this. Certainly one of these is scale. A church building should not overwhelm or impress the beholder as if one enters merely to be a passive spectator. Large monumental public spaces often have that effect. A church, though, is for people who will participate in a common activity—worship. Indeed, if any word is central in our thinking about worship today, it is *participation*. Vatican II's call for "that full, conscious, and active participation" of the whole community could well be the slogan for all the changes we have seen in worship in the last twenty years. Christians of every tradition have used "participation" as a key criterion for evaluating everything about worship, including its architectural setting. As we look to the future, *participation* may have even broader meanings than we now realize; it probably will include the whole worshiping community, from infants to the elderly, in fuller involvement.

Another way of saying this in terms of space is that there is the need to convey a sense of *intimacy*. Intimacy fosters a sense of participation. Its opposites are isolation and detachment. When we feel we are actors on stage, we are more likely to play our parts with gusto than when we see ourselves simply as spectators. Many factors besides that of scale contribute to intimacy. The question of acoustics is important; sound makes a big difference. It can behave so one thinks one is singing alone or give the impression of the support of many voices. Art is another factor that can humanize space and make us feel a part of what goes on in it. Intimacy makes us feel we belong, that we are a part of the service, not mere spectators or auditors. Only then can we experience participation to the fullest extent.

In this chapter we shall be examining those spaces that the community of faith uses on all occasions. These spaces are found in the churches and meetinghouses of every Christian tradition, including groups such as Quakers who have no altar-table, pulpit, or font. Three spaces are common to all church buildings, and we shall start with those. Subsequent chapters will explore the spaces necessary for each of the various occasions for worship in Christian communities.

Analysis of Functions

In order to analyze the way anything works, it is often useful to divide it into *individual components so* that each can be analyzed in turn. This is certainly the case with church architecture, especially when we are concerned with how it functions as the setting for Christian worship. Obviously, all the parts of a building are interrelated, but the mind cannot examine at the same time all the ways every part functions. So we must treat them as discrete components, realizing they do not exist in isolation but always as parts of the whole. Even then the sum is much more than just a total of isolated parts.

Each church consists of six distinct spaces: gathering space, movement space, congregational space, choir space, altar-table space, and baptismal space. In addition, there are three essential liturgical centers or furnishings: altar-table, baptismal font or pool, pulpit; and frequently subsidiary furnishings, such as lectern, prayer desk, communion rails, and clergy seating. In speaking of the altar-table, we shall emphasize that it is both altar and table. Our concern in this chapter is with the spaces used for gathering, movement, and congregational seating.

In order to analyze how space works in worship, it is useful to visualize space by means of floor plans. Essentially, this means looking down as if the roof were off and the walls were represented by solid lines, with openings for doors. We are not concerned with elaborate and detailed floor plans but with simplified schemes which can help us visualize the limits of individual spaces, the location of liturgical furnishings, and how the various spaces and furnishings relate to one another. In similar fashion, one might examine a private home to see how the dining room relates to the kitchen and how the stove, refrigerator, and sink relate to one another. One can then have a fairly good idea of how much movement is required to cook and serve a meal. If one must pass through another room to go from the kitchen to the dining room, or if the stove is twenty feet from the sink, there are functional problems to be resolved. The function of space can also be analyzed this way in worship. Our best analytical tool is a floor plan.

For our purposes, it is useful to sketch simple floor plans, using letters to designate liturgical centers:

4

P — pulpit
A — altar-table
B — baptismal font or pool
G — gathering space
C — choir space

Additionally:

- Congregational seating is indicated by parallel lines representing pews or chairs.
- Space surrounding the altar-table or the baptismal font or pool may be indicated by a circle around the appropriate letter.
- Movement space may be suggested by arrows indicating the usual directions of movement.

Other letters and symbols may be added as needed. A simple arrangement could be indicated in this way (see Fig. 1).

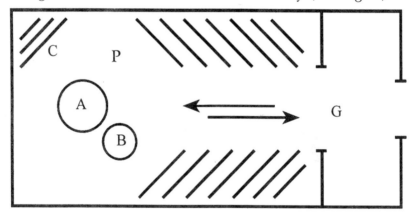

Figure 1

The purpose of such floor plans is not to design new or renovated buildings but simply to analyze the function in worship of various spaces in either projected or existing buildings. The architect designs space; it is the congregation's responsibility to think through how the space it is purchasing or renovating will function as an essential agent in forming its worship life. Sketching such floor plans can be an essential exercise in understanding how any building shapes the life of the community of faith. The floor plan gives graphic visibility to the spatial realities with which we must live. Thus it is a most helpful analytical tool for raising the question: What goes on here?

One general comment should be made before we analyze specific spaces: Christian worship is not an esoteric, devious affair; usually the most simple, direct, utilitarian approach is best. The finest church buildings in every era have sought to provide the simplest and most useful setting for worship. This means that the architecture serves the function and is not a monument unto itself. The Christian community gathers not to admire its building but to use the structure. It is not a community of tourists from afar, viewing something in which it never shares. The Christian community must build simply and directly for its own needs in worship. Anything beyond that is conspicuous consumption and contrary to the essence of Christianity.

Frequently, when Christians take most seriously that which is simple and direct, eschewing the monumental or purely decorative, the resulting building has the greatest aesthetic appeal. The dictum of architect Ludwig Mies van der Rohe, "Less is more," has much to say to church builders.

We shall turn, then, to the spaces used by the whole congregation on all occasions; spaces for gathering, movement, and congregational seating.

Gathering Space

In recent years, much concern has been shown regarding gathering space. The reasons for this reveal much about Christian worship itself.

The Christian community needs to assemble in order to worship together. Indeed, this act of coming together may be the most important single thing that happens on Sunday morning. The coming together of those called out from the world is essential to forming the body of Christ. We have seen this act all too often as simply utilitarian,

6

something necessary but not important. When Christians assemble for worship, they are doing something the rest of the world cannot do or even understand—forming the body of their risen Lord present on earth in their midst. Dire consequences result, as Paul reminds us, when the gathered community fails to recognize whose body it is and falls into bickering and greed (1 Cor. 11:29).

Gathering together to form the body of Christ, then, is an essential act of Christian worship because it unites us as Christ's body on earth. This means a temporary stepping out of the world in order to participate for a time in the Church as an advance vision of God's kingdom. It also means a coming together to share in the gifts of the Holy Spirit, manifest among God's people in the holy Church. As Quaker theologian Robert Barclay expressed it, "Many candles lighted and put in one place do greatly augment the light, and make it more to shine forth."[1] Assembly is essential to being the Church.

At one time the gathering of Christians was a highly dangerous act in defiance of civil authority, often resulting in martyrdom. Although the Roman empire cared little what Christians did or what they believed, it was determined to prevent their assembling because it knew the church would die out if it did not meet. Even within a free society, gathering as the Church is a political act, proclaiming allegiance to another kingdom.

In the New Testament, the Christian gathering place is once spoken of as a *synagogue* (James 2:2). The Puritans used the term *meetinghouse* for their building, using *church* only for the people who convened in the meetinghouse. There is a double meaning in this term *meetinghouse;* not only do we meet God when we come to worship, but first we meet our neighbor. The vertical God-human encounter occurs in the midst of a horizontal, human-human encounter. Some key words for this activity are gathering, coming together, assembling, congregating, convening, conferring. One thing is clear — Christians must come together to worship as the body of Christ.

If assembling is so important, it is a bit surprising that there is so little evidence of that in most churches built in the not-so-distant past. Other than a necessary narthex or vestibule, there seems to have been little thought given to the way space shapes the experience of gathering together to form a worshiping community. The usual pattern for most worshipers is a beeline from the parking lot, often through a side entrance, to the pew, moving from the private space of the car to the public space of the pew, with little or no experience of the coming together of a community. Sometimes one can go from car to pew without meeting other worshipers at all.

Recent buildings demonstrate a much greater concern with the role of the church building itself in shaping the experience of forming a worshiping community. These buildings are based on the premise that gathering is an important act of worship in itself and that worship begins when the first person arrives at church. The most recent United Methodist and Presbyterian services call attention to this by listing "gathering" or "gathering of the people" as the first act in the order of worship. All churches are giving serious thought to ways the arrangement of space shapes the experience of assembling for worship.

This implies a need to conceive of space, both outside the building and within it, as a processional path by which members of the community converge to worship together. Usually the church has no control over land beyond its property lines, although zoning laws often prohibit certain types of businesses within specified distances from churches. But the church can plan the experience of what transpires on its own land. Our chief concern is to bring people together so they can meet face to face as they prepare to meet their God. One useful image is that of many paths converging on a common clearing in the forest.

Hospitality is a fundamental aspect of all that happens in the gathering space, both inside and outside the building. These spaces need to welcome both the stranger and the person familiar with the place and people. Monumental and imposing forms may be awesome and impressive to the passerby but they do not generally attract and invite people to enter. Human-scaled spaces call us to come inside, especially when a covered entrance suggests shelter. On the other hand, a chain-link fence, which shelters no one, is the opposite of hospitality. Inside, low ceilings, art work, and furnishings on a human scale can enhance the sense of welcome. By its very nature, a Christian church is committed to growth through welcoming others. Gathering space must help proclaim: We want you to be one with us.

Several practical details should be remembered in planning gathering space. First of all, the experience of gathering involves exterior space as well as that inside the building. Since most people in America come to church by car, the location of parking space is immensely important. Are parking lots designed to lead to a common entrance? One can plan multiple parking lots that lead to such an entrance, rather than to back-door shortcuts.

The quality of the path that leads from parking to entrance is immensely important. Frequently, the experience of processing to the church can be enhanced by landscaping such as a double row of trees or shrubs. The rhythms of alternating light and shadow on such plants lead one forward. The paving of the paths must be safe in the dark but can be interesting and inviting. Lighting is necessary for evening meetings.

Some kind of enclosure such as walls or hedges can create a gathering place on the exterior of the building. Many ancient churches had an atrium, or forecourt, where Christians assembled before entering the church, forming the transition from the world to the gathered assembly. Often these forecourts made provision for a symbolic washing of hands as the people withdrew from the world. Many medieval churches were entered through a porch which served both sacred and secular functions as a gathering place for ratifying contracts in the sight of God. Until recent times churches were surrounded by graveyards, where the church on earth met among reminders of the church in heaven.

All this is to say that what intervenes between car door and church door is an essential preparation for what happens once we are inside the building. Exterior space may require less money for construction but nevertheless requires much thought in the design process. The landscape architect can make an important contribution here.

Gathering space on the interior deserves special consideration. Our concern here is to help form a community of people whose worship together is not that of strangers but of people who can pray for and with one another because they share their joys and sorrows. This space, all too often neglected and viewed simply as a foyer or vestibule, yet has much to do with the quality of worship inside the main worship area. Here an important part of forming the body of Christ takes place in the informal activities of conversation, greeting, hand shaking, and so on. How human our worship is!

How can we design this space so that it enhances the experience of gathering? We have mentioned the dimension of hospitality, a quality we associate with homes, especially when entertaining, and since many of the same features are operative here, it may be helpful to think of this space in domestic terms. Intimacy, comfort, informality, fellowship—all are qualities that adhere to hospitable surroundings. There must be ample space to stand or sit so people can greet each other without feeling pressured to get out of the way immediately so others can enter. This requires far more space than generally has been provided in the narthex.

Many possibilities are reflected in recent buildings. Architect Edward Sövik often designs what he calls a concourse, furnishing it with the kind of chairs and tables associated with ice-cream parlors. The purpose is to lure people to sit and talk before and after services.[2] These have often had the effect of inducing people to come earlier and stay after the service. Frank Kacmarcik, as designer and consultant, has provided a hospitable outdoor "gathering place" at St. Peter's Church in Saratoga Springs, New York.

This intimate space is between three buildings, with a wall of enclosure on the street side and an overhead canopy of tree limbs. He has also designed an interior gathering place surrounding the baptismal pool at St. Elizabeth Seton Church, Carmel, Indiana.

Concern must be shown for the amenities of such space. In most climates, cloakrooms will be necessary for people to shed and hang winter coats and rain gear. Toilets must be conveniently located and identified. It may be desirable to provide a nook where coffee, punch, and light food can be prepared and served. Sometimes storage space for medical-emergency equipment is needed.

Movement Space

The community's movement does not end once it has reached the gathering space. Usually this space is separated from the main worship room by exterior or interior walls so that the coming together of the community happens in a distinct space where the focus is on gathering. But once they have assembled, it is necessary for people to move to the places, usually pews or chairs, which they will occupy for the main portion of the service. They now enter another kind of space: movement space.

Throughout most of the history of Christian worship, the major portion of the interior space of the building was movement space. There were no pews or chairs. Not until the fourteenth century did seating gradually encroach upon the open space where the congregation stood and walked about during worship. Until that time, the people were on their feet and could go wherever something was happening, whether it was to cluster about the pulpit or get a better view of the altar-table, as they still do in many Orthodox and Oriental churches. The congregation was mobile and the interior of the church was not regimented into fixed rows of inflexible pews.

In the late Middle Ages the congregation sat down on the job and there was a drastic change in Christian worship—perhaps the most important in history. People, in effect, became custodians of individual spaces which they occupied throughout the service, and social distinctions made some spaces more privileged than others. This change from a mobile congregation to a sedentary one remains a major challenge to those who plan and conduct worship. Nonetheless, movement is still an important part of Christian worship in every tradition, although not as conspicuously so as before pews occupied most of the territory. In planning church buildings, the importance of movement as an essential part of worship itself should not be overlooked. Movement from place to place is not simply a matter of convenience; it is an important ingredient of worship. Literally, Christians worship with their whole bodies, including their feet.

Movement space, then, is worship space, and it functions in a variety of ways, all of which should be considered in planning churches. This space functions most obviously in the coming and going of the congregation as people arrive to take their places in the pews or chairs as the service begins, and leave as it ends. This means that a first requirement of movement space is access to seating. If pews are too long and remote from movement space, there are likely to be areas rarely occupied simply because of difficulty of access. In general, aisles should take one within five seats of any seat in the church, or too much difficulty in climbing over people will make interior seating unusable.

Movement space is used also in various acts of offering. Ushers, in many churches, take up an offering of money and bring it to the front of the church. For this, access to all the seating is necessary. On some occasions the entire congregation may bring tithes and offerings to the altar-table. Frequently, bread and wine are placed on a table at the entrance to the church and brought forward during the offertory in preparation for the Lord's Supper.

In many churches those receiving communion move from their seats to the communion rail or communion stations, where they receive the bread and wine as they kneel or stand. The act of going forward to receive communion is, in itself, an eloquent statement of both self-offering and going to receive a gift. In some cases the people may go forward in groups to sit about the altar-table. Where communion in the pews is practiced, there needs to be access for the servers to reach each row of pews.

Another type of movement occurs when there is a baptism, confirmation, or reception into church membership. People from the congregation must have access to the baptismal font or pool when a baptism is celebrated (cf. chap. 4).

Various processions are also part of worship. How does the choir get in and out of the choir space? All too often, inadequate space has necessitated a major performance just to get the choir members into their places. It must arrive and leave somehow, so care must be exercised that this can be done conveniently and unobtrusively rather than consuming five minutes of the service. One needs to work out, on a floor plan, the movement from choir room to choir space, or every Sunday this lack of oversight will be regretted.

On some occasions, such as Passion/Palm Sunday, the whole congregation may process. Usually this works best around the periphery of the building. The Roman Catholic Cathedral in Burlington, Vermont, is a good example of a building which facilitates such movement. Occasionally outdoor space is used for congregational processions, although this risks the uncertainty of the weather. The problems involved are how to get people out of their seats, into the aisles, moving without running into people coming from the opposite direction, and back into their seats. In some buildings, where space to enable this has not been planned, such movement is very nearly impossible; in others it is quite feasible.

Highly visible acts in most weddings are the procession of the bride and the recession of the married couple. A central aisle is usually preferred so that all can see, but other routes are possible (cf. chap. 5). It should be remembered that these two ritual movements testify to an important change for the individuals concerned, and space must be designed accordingly.

Other demands for movement space are made by funerals. Often the casket is brought in during the service; usually it is carried out afterward, frequently by pallbearers on each side. This dictates a minimum width for one aisle. A place for the casket to rest during the service must also be considered in planning this space.

Revivalism discovered that to move people spiritually, you must move them physically. In some churches people come forward for altar prayers; this necessitates both accessibility and a place to kneel. Children may come forward for special lessons or prayers. The congregation may move about for passing the peace. Dramatic or dance performances may be a part of worship. Movement space may be necessary also for those who come forward to renew or reaffirm their baptism, or to offer themselves in commitment or some new form of Christian discipleship. The space between the first pew and the communion rail or platform is used in a variety of ways and should be of ample width.

Some practical consequences of these various types of movement should be clear. Movement is not extraneous to worship, but an integral part of it. Space designed for movement is not waste space to be kept as small as possible; it is important worship space, though temporary seating may encroach upon it at times.

Congregational Space

The third type of space used by the whole community at every service is congregational space. In modern churches this is filled with seating either pews or chairs or benches—

so it is indeed seating space. But it is not the only seating space, since seating is provided elsewhere for choir and clergy. Furthermore, it would not be entirely appropriate to call this area *seating* space, since it is also the place where the congregation worships while standing and kneeling. Congregational space is the location where one sits, stands, or kneels in order to concentrate on seeing, hearing, speaking, singing, and making gestures that do not require much movement (such as a handclasp).

If one word can describe this space, it is *participation* space. Here the gathered congregation worships—not as a passive audience, but fully and actively involved. However, in many cases the greatest barrier to full participation is architecture. The arrangement of space in some churches makes participation by all difficult because of inadequate sight lines, remoteness of location, poor acoustics, bad lighting, and other factors. Hence an important part of liturgical reform is concern to eliminate all barriers to participation in congregational space.

A primary concern in thinking about this space is its configuration. Since in almost all cases it is by far the largest space in the building, some very important decisions must be made in shaping it. In the context of emphasis on participation, this means that many solutions of the past are no longer satisfactory. The least satisfactory is the longitudinal, or basilican plan, with the congregation stretched out in a long tunnel-like nave:

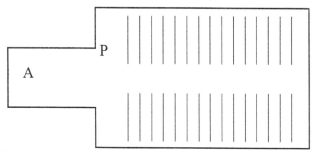

Figure 2

15

Even when there are acceptable sight lines and the acoustics are adequate, such buildings leave those in the rear in a passive role, suggesting that the action is up front. It is not possible here to discuss the historical reason for choosing other plans in the Reformation era and the subsequent experimentation that continued for three centuries.[3] Suffice it to say that many past attempts at alternative shapes have inspired recent efforts to find new ways to form this congregational space.

Basically, newer shapes tend to be centralized rather than longitudinal; an effort is being made to bring the congregation as close as possible to such liturgical centers as pulpit, altar-table, and baptismal font or pool. In some cases, congregational space has been wrapped around the altar-table space, and it has been found possible to seat a fairly large congregation in eight rows of pews, provided this space is well planned. Any such design necessitates compromises between the best arrangements for preaching and those for the Lord's Supper. Such trade-offs usually lead to a middle course between a small segment of a circle (in which the preaching sight lines are most direct) and a half circle or even wider segment (in which the congregational space surrounds the altar-table). These needs will be discussed in more detail in chapters 2 and 3; these simplified floor plans show some of the possibilities:

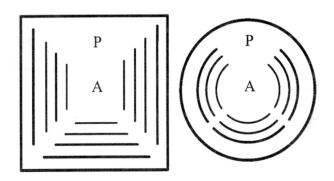

Figure 3

In short, there is no simple answer to the question of what shape works best for congregational space today, although there does seem to be consensus that the long nave is not acceptable. Some congregations have made drastic efforts to reshape space to accommodate worship today. In a number of cases, this has involved renovating a longitudinal-type building by walling off the former chancel area and placing the altar-table and pulpit in the middle of a long side:

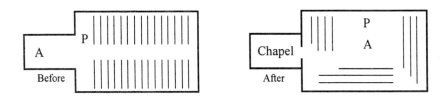

Figure 4

Such efforts may require major surgery, but often have produced buildings that have gained new usefulness by supporting current understandings of Christian worship rather than fighting them. The task of designing new buildings is no less arduous, but it is free from some of the obstacles of starting with existing space. In both cases, we are trying to avoid long receding space in favor of space that emphasizes congregational participation to the fullest degree.

A number of practical concerns arise. Since congregational space is filled with seating, we should note current developments. Until recent decades, most American churches were filled with fixed pews; this limited us to a single configuration of people, namely, in parallel rows. The building was always the same, no matter the number of people present or the occasion. The 1960s, a period of massive changes in worship, showed the need for other possibilities. This led to the removal of pews in a number of churches and the substitution of movable seating that was attractive and comfortable. In this way, many arrangements became possible and the community was able to shape congregational space around the people or the occasion.

Great advantages were realized in the flexibility thus gained. A church with pews for two hundred people will seem half empty if only one hundred show up for a service. When this same space is set up to seat one hundred, people will say that "there were so many people present they had to bring in extra seats!" Movable seating can be set up into different configurations for weddings, baptisms, the antiphonal recitation of a daily office, and other occasions. Such seating can reflect the worship rather than dictate to it.

Although there are certainly advantages to flexibility, we have lived long enough with movable seating to realize that there are certain disadvantages, too. In comfort and attractiveness, chairs should be equal to pews. Indeed, they have been preferred in many European cathedrals. We are not talking about inexpensive folding chairs, but attractive single-unit seats. Such seating is as costly as pews of equal quality. Anyone who buys hardwood furniture today knows that quality is not cheap. Furniture that is not securely anchored can sometimes be dangerous for those with handicapping conditions and the infirm, who may rely on it for support when sitting down and rising. Furthermore, such seating should be capable of being ganged (firmly linked together) because of local fire codes, and it should be stackable so as to conserve space. For this, ample storage room must be available.

Flexibility has many advantages but it is also demanding. Someone must have the time and incentive to set up the building for varying types of services. Frequently, the effort becomes too much and the chairs are left in the same arrangement continually, thus voiding their greatest advantage, flexibility. Care must be taken also that the chairs are kept in an orderly fashion so the building does not look sloppy and ill-cared for. Also, the use of chairs is nearly impossible with sloping floors. Because of these considerations, planning for congregational space must weigh carefully the relative advantages of fixed and movable seating. A few compromises are possible. Some churches have certain areas in fixed seating (pews) and other areas (those less likely to be used or those for overflow seating) where chairs are provided. One can thus have limited flexibility with both fixed and movable seating. Also available are short pews which seat about four people and are not fixed to the floor. These can be moved when necessary but usually stay in the same place.

Seating is an expensive and permanent purchase. Careful decisions must be made after weighing all the alternatives. Some churches have gained much more use from their space by substituting movable seating for pews; they would argue that flexibility may pay for itself in avoiding further building. But flexibility does involve staff or volunteer time to make it work effectively, and these are not always available or affordable.

In some churches kneelers are considered a necessity, though recently there has been a move to more prayer in a standing posture. Although the use of kneelers has not been eliminated, the length of time used has shortened in most services. Fixed kneelers may be hinged to pews, or individual hassocks may be placed beneath pews or chairs or hung from hooks. If the congregation does use kneelers, more space will be required between rows of pews or chairs, which lessens seating capacity to some extent.

One of the hallmarks of the modern church may be the crowded hymnal rack. As service books and hymnals have proliferated, more and more paperback volumes seem to be stuffed into the space provided. With more stability and consolidation in our worship, their species are not likely to multiply as fast, but it still will be necessary to provide ample space for book storage on pews or chairs — preferably room for two books per individual. Some churches also require holders for communion glasses or racks for cards of various sorts.

Good sight lines cannot be overemphasized. The ability to see those leading the worship is usually enhanced by elevation of the pulpit and altar-table space, although when this height is excessive it becomes a visual barrier, since it is necessary for those near the front to hold their heads at an awkward angle. Of course, if every part of the congregational space is close enough to pulpit and altar-table, the problem should be minimal.

Another solution is a sloping floor, which, in larger buildings, may be desirable. But serious problems are attached to such a solution. We wish to avoid sloping floors when they necessitate additional exterior or interior stairways. These can pose grave difficulties for those with disabilities, and there are economic factors to be considered, since sloping floors usually involve additional structural costs. Such floors also are likely to increase the cost of pews, each of which must match the angle of incline. And of course, they make movable seating almost impossible. In some cases, sloping floors may be the best solution to making what happens at pulpit and altar-table visible to everyone, but all alternatives to this solution ought to be weighed carefully first.

Since congregational space is the predominant space in most churches, it should not be surprising that much time and concern should go into decisions about it. But hardly any other decisions will have such an important impact on the purpose for which the building is used. The design of this space can make full participation in worship either a reality commonly achieved or a rarity usually sought in vain. These decisions must not be made in haste but with care for every aspect.

Two

A PLACE FOR THE
SERVICE OF THE WORD

We turn now to examine the distinct types of services in the repertoire of Christian worship and to investigate how the church building functions in each of them. This and the next four chapters will describe the demands of each type of service and how the building can best provide that space. Church music will receive a separate treatment in similar fashion.

The Service of the Word

We begin by looking at the most common type of service, the service of the Word. Unfortunately, this name will mean little to most people because this type of service goes by so many other names that it is necessary to find a neutral term. Names for this service vary between, and even within, denominations: morning worship, morning order, Lord's Day service, divine worship, antecommunion, foremass, synaxis, preaching service, or proclamation of the Word of God. By whatever name, we are talking about the usual Sunday service or preaching service for most Protestants, and the first part of the Mass or Lord's Supper for Roman Catholics, Episcopalians, and many Protestants. The service of the Word is common to virtually all churches except some in the Quaker tradition.

Despite the confusion about a common name, the contents are remarkably similar from denomination to denomination. This service (or portion of a service) centers around the proclamation of the Word of God through the reading of Scripture and the preaching. Interspersed with the readings may be psalms, canticles, hymns, anthems, or various congregational responses. In addition, prayers and other acts of worship precede and follow the central proclamation of the Word.

The Christian community comes together to hear the Word of God. This divine Word is heard in the rehearsing of the corporate memories which make the community one, namely, those memories we know as Scripture. The readings from the Bible remind the community of what God has done for it in times past and promises to do in the present and future. Through music and preaching, these memories are opened for the congregation to reflect upon, so that the meanings of those acts of God commemorated in the readings maybe applied to the circumstances of current life. And praying in this context of God's work gives the worshipers hope to see God's work continuing in the present.

In reading and preaching from the Bible, both the community's history as the people of God and its future are declared. Each service of the Word is a service of re-membering, in which the community refreshes its memory about what God has done for it, culminating in the work of Christ. But the God whose works shape the corporate memories is also present now in worship and acts in and through the recalling of God's past work. This same God is addressed in prayer, petitioning for daily bread and inter-ceding for those in need and distress.

Central in the service of the Word is the Christian community's dialogue with God through the medium of spoken words. God speaks to the community by readings from Scripture and the sermon, and the community speaks to God through psalms, canticles, hymns, and anthems. In this spoken and sung encounter with God, hearing is para-mount. Indeed, sometimes the phrase "Hear the Word of God" is exclaimed. We are dealing with a speech-event, and this type of worship is heavily dependent upon language spoken and heard.

This should not conceal from us the fact that it is also highly visual. It is crucial that the speaker be seen and not seem to be a disembodied voice. The source of sound, even if a loudspeaker, should be as closely identified with the visible individual as possible. The person who speaks does so not only with the mouth but with the entire body. One cannot read a Scripture lesson without also interpreting it, and much interpretation comes through body language. The reader or preacher must be fully present to the congregation to be the most effective communicator. Fullness of presence demands both visibility and audibility. In some churches there are actions related to the reading of Scripture, such as carrying the Bible into worship in the entrance procession, moving the Bible in order to read from it, or a gospel procession, all of which demand visibility in order to communicate.

Although its central focus is on reading and preaching, the service of the Word also includes other elements which must be considered in any planning of worship space. In most cases there is an *entrance rite*. This usually includes the gathering of the community, a procession of choir and clergy, the greeting by the presider, a hymn of praise, various opening prayers, and sometimes other acts of praise. Taken together, these necessitate a number of different spaces besides those described in chapter 1.

If the presider addresses the congregation with a greeting, he or she will usually stand facing the congregation, either in the pulpit, at the presider's chair, or in space we shall call "before the altar table"—that is, the space between the altar-table and the people. (We shall call the space on the opposite side "behind the altar-table.") The presider may stand before the altar-table during such actions as greeting, announcements, and benediction. In some traditions, the minister approaches the altar-table itself at this time; in others, at a subsequent time. The first distinct need is space before the altar-table.

At the heart of the service is the *reading and preaching of God's Word*, usually with musical interludes. The congrega-

tion may stand to sing and to hear the gospel but movement virtually ceases, except for those few who go to the
pulpit to read or preach. Attention is focused on one spot,
the pulpit, for up to half the service.

Reading and preaching are usually followed by various
forms of *responses to the Word*. These will vary from denomination to denomination and from week to week but
frequently include a creed, or hymn, or prayer, or invitation. From what spot will these acts of worship be led? The
pulpit is one possibility, the presider's chair another, before the altar-table yet another. Often at this time, baptisms,
confirmations, and the welcoming of people into the local
congregation occur. (We shall discuss appropriate spaces
for these actions in chap. 4.)

Frequently, this part of the service of the Word consists of prayers for others, prayers of petition, and a prayer
of confession. Some of these may be led by members of the
congregation. If so, will they remain in the pews, stand in
the aisle, or come forward to the front of the church? Will
it be necessary to have a portable microphone so those leading prayer can be heard? Will the minister repeat the
intercessions so all can hear? Audibility is frequently a problem at this point and demands careful planning. If the
presider leads all these prayers, alone or in unison, where
can he or she best be heard? Some will use the pulpit, others may prefer to stand before or behind the altar-table.
Declaration of pardon may be a clerical act, pronounced
standing and facing the congregation. From what location
can this best be heard and seen as a pronouncement of God's
will to forgive?

In many churches, there is a passing of the peace at
this point or elsewhere in the service. This should not necessitate much movement on the part of the congregation,
but the clergy may need quick access to the first row of
pews. Frequently, announcements are made in an informal
way either by clergy or members of the congregation. This
may involve need for sound amplification.

Often an offering is received at this time, and a seemly way to hand over the money must be found. This may indicate a need for wide steps to the altar-table if many ushers are involved. When the Eucharist is not celebrated, prayers of thanksgiving may be offered from behind the altar-table. Almost always there is a brief *closing rite.* This may involve prayers, a hymn, a dismissal and benediction, a choir or clergy recession, and the scattering of the congregation. Here again space for the presider to stand facing the congregation, usually before the altar-table, is necessary. And again, movement space and gathering space function as the community leaves.

If anything, this brief excursion through the service of the Word should remind us how many different spaces and centers are utilized. How well they function depends largely upon how carefully the needs of the congregation have been thought through and expressed in order that an architect can provide for them. It is helpful to take the usual Sunday morning order of worship as found in the bulletin or service book and ask these questions of each item: Who does this? How do we do it? Where can it best be done? How do we do it differently on special occasions? Then it is possible to list what is needed for the service of the Word.

Places for the Word

Several distinct spaces and centers are needed for the service of the Word. We shall focus on the three that are uniquely important in this type of worship, although they function in many other types: pulpit, presider's chair, and space before the altar-table. (We shall use the word *pulpit;* some liturgical scholars call it an *ambo.*)

Several important considerations about the design and location of the pulpit have major impact on the conduct and experience of the service of the Word. All these revolve around its primary function as the center for the reading and preaching of God's Word, as well as its possible use as a place from which other portions of this service are led.

In many present-day churches, there are both a pulpit and a lectern. Some important decisions must be made about the desirability of retaining the lectern when renovating, or of including one in a new building. Present trends have moved away from the presence of both a lectern and a pulpit. The lectern, as now found in many Protestant churches, is a relic of a Victorian version of medieval church architecture. The lectern made good functional sense for medieval monks in their daily services. In the nineteenth century it came to replace part of a combined liturgical center (pulpit, reading desk, and clerk's desk). As an independent entity, its chief architectural function seemed to be to balance the pulpit on the other side of the chancel. As a liturgical center, it was used for reading the lessons but ignored for preaching the sermon. A separate lectern makes little historical sense today.

Theologically, the split between pulpit and lectern makes even less sense. With the widespread use of the lectionary and a move to more exegetical preaching, the trend is to make the unity of God's Word found in Scripture and preaching more obvious. The separate lectern and pulpit proclaim a distinction we are trying to avoid rather than underscore. To read God's Word from one place (the lectern) and then go elsewhere (the pulpit) to open the Scriptures to our understanding is bad theology and a counterproductive effort.

Emphasis on what is essential and avoidance of nonessentials makes a stronger architectural and liturgical statement. There is nothing especially laudable about symmetry (despite the Victorians). Some churches have replaced the lectern with a baptismal font, thus obtaining a more functional balance. At any rate, money spent on a lectern can be used for much better purposes.

There are several options as to the design of the pulpit. Historically, there has been a vast array of possibilities, from a small reading stand to a massive tub pulpit in which the preacher stood. The "wineglass" pulpit which enclosed the preacher in the Georgian meetinghouse was superseded, in many instances, by a desk-type pulpit on a platform, where evangelical preachers could roam from side to side. Recent preferences have been more modest structures simply large enough to hold the Bible and the preacher's notes or manuscript. Basically, the focus is the shelf, usually sloping a bit, designed to hold book and manuscript; the rest of the pulpit is simply a support. For convenience, there may be concealed shelves to hold other books from which the preacher may quote, a glass of water, and a clock. Some preachers prefer a movable pulpit, which dictates that it be of modest size. There are, however, dangers that such pulpits may look too provisional and the placement may be too casual.

The scale of the pulpit is an important concern. Recent years have seen a turning away from monumental pulpits which foster the idea that the preaching is "six feet above contradiction." There has been a desire to avoid undue elevation of the preacher (as much as twelve feet in some colonial churches) and preaching has become a less domineering and more democratic activity. At the same time, sufficient height is necessary so that the preacher is visible from the back of the church. Careful planning will ensure that there is enough elevation for full visibility without undue height. Pulpits should be seen as serving, not as dominating, the Word of God.

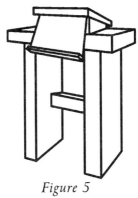

Figure 5

A close visual association between the Bible (lectionary or Gospel book) itself and the act of preaching is highly desirable. Frequently this is accomplished by having a small shelf on the front of the pulpit, where the Bible is placed except during the time it is being read (see Fig. 5). The action of moving the Bible onto the top of the pulpit for the readings and then returning it to view just before the sermon can be an eloquent statement of the connection between preaching and reading of Scripture. The place for the Bible is the pulpit, where it is used, rather than on the altar-table where it has no function.

In designing a pulpit with a shelf to show the Bible, it should be kept in mind that books do not look their best when open in an upright position and that a pulpit Bible should be well-bound and attractive.

A few practical details should be noted. Since the height of preachers varies, it is necessary that the desk part of the pulpit be adjustable or that a movable platform be placed where the preacher stands. Lighting is important but should be carefully designed so it does not cause shadows on the face of the preacher. Bad lighting can make even the most benign of preachers look satanic. If a microphone is necessary, it should be as inconspicuous as possible, since an attractive microphone does not seem to exist. Frequently a microphone that clips onto the preacher's garment is preferable.

The location of the pulpit depends on the arrangement of the congregational space and choir space. The preacher needs to be able to see everyone to whom he or she is preaching, including the choir members. A trite but convenient slogan instructs: Don't preach until you see the whites of their eyes. The preacher must watch faces as well as notes, and the congregation needs to see the preacher's face and hands. We shall return to this problem of pulpit location shortly.

The second liturgical center, the presider's chair, is considerably more problematic. Everyone agrees on the need for a pulpit to hold the Bible and serve as the locus of reading and preaching. That is not subject to question, whatever the denomination.

But the presider's chair as a prominent liturgical center is a new development in that it represents a new approach for Roman Catholics in their attempt to declericalize worship. The rationale for making the presider's chair a prominent liturgical center is that when the presider is not standing, he or she is delegating the leadership of worship to readers, leaders of prayer, or musicians. This may seem a token move but it is significant in its recognition that many people share in the leadership of worship. Thus, for Roman Catholics, the importance of the presider's chair is not to be missed. It is not meant to be a throne, but a rather modest seat fully visible to the entire assembly.

For many Protestants, on the other hand, the presider's chair is all too painful a memory, and thousands of renovations have sought to remove it. The legacy from the nineteenth century was usually three large chairs on a platform facing the congregation: a central one (the presider's chair), a chair for the visiting preacher, and a chair for the song leader. Large, ornate, and ugly, they are the first targets of renovations, and clergy today usually end up in some discrete form of choir stall, facing the center of the platform rather than the congregation. Perhaps this is just compensation for a position once too obtrusive, too dominant, and much too ugly.

What value is there for Roman Catholics in the Protestant experience with clergy seating? And is the new Roman Catholic arrangement simply a passing phase? These are hard questions to sort out definitively; the lessons here are ultimately concerns about social control. Ironically, adding a chair for Roman Catholic priests can represent a lessening of social control, whereas concealing the chair for Protestant clergy may have the same impact. Of course, not all clergy, Roman Catholic or Protestant, are willing to move to a leadership style not based on domination, and some may insist upon being on their feet throughout the entire service. In sitting down, one usually is delegating the leadership role. Building committees and clergy will need to ask themselves some hard questions about how dominating their minister or priest should be in worship, before they proceed to discuss clergy seating. Very important issues of who "does" the service of worship arise at this point.

In any case, some practical problems must be faced. There always will be a need for clergy seating. Some may prefer stalls similar to those the choir occupies, or perhaps a part of the choir space. In a more radical approach, the minister could sit with his or her family in congregational space when others are speaking or singing. This is feasible only in rather small buildings since it involves too much moving about and might prove distracting. Probably better are modest movable chairs, which may or may not face the congregation.

In addition, it must be recognized that a number of leaders may need to be seated. Frequently, several ministers or priests play various roles in each service, although one usually presides. In some traditions, seating must be provided for elders or deacons who fulfill important roles, especially at the Lord's Supper. Seating often is necessary for lay readers, prayer leaders, acolytes, music leaders, and others. One must determine how many such persons are usually present and where they can be best situated to do what they do.

A case can be made for a modest presider's chair that is distinctive from the others and used as one of the centers for leadership of the service of the Word. It definitely should be a chair, not a throne with a high back or canopy. Adequate lighting is required, and provision may be necessary for a microphone connection nearby.

In Episcopal parish churches in this country, there has been a long tradition of a bishop's chair, which is occupied by the bishop on the occasion of visitation. Usually this chair is impressive but does not face the congregation; it can be ignored when vacant. This practice seems largely confined to this country, and the bishop's chair probably could be superseded by a presider's chair, which the bishop could occupy.

It should be kept in mind that the presider's chair, especially when vacant, is not a symbol of Word or sacrament, as are pulpit and baptismal font or pool. It should not compete with these for visual attention. The symbol is the person who ministers, and that person is not tied to the chair or to any single location. An empty chair means nothing; a pulpit holds the Bible, the font contains water, and both these contents are put to sacred use. But a modest presider's chair may be a sign of a move to a more participatory style of worship, something that should be welcomed by Protestant and Roman Catholic communities alike.

The third concern is altar-table space, especially that space before the altar-table. This is the natural place for the person leading worship to greet the congregation, make announcements, or receive the offering, as we have said. In short, in this location, the leader speaks to the congregation both in dialogue and in spoken rubrics, such as "Let us offer one another signs of reconciliation and love." It may also be the practice to speak to God in prayer, especially in the opening prayers, from this space. (In most Roman Catholic churches, such greetings, prayers, and announcements take place at the presider's chair.)

In some churches, on occasion, a litany desk, a portable prayer desk, may be placed at this location so that the minister may kneel while leading the congregation in a litany. If intercessors come from the congregation, they may use this space to lead in prayer, and during services of healing, this space will be used.

Several requirements are indicated. Space before the altar-table must be accessible directly from the congregational space. Where there are steps, they should extend across the entire front of this area in order to accommodate the many occasions when several people move into this location. These steps should face the congregation rather than ascend the platform from the side. Visually, this is an important sign of hospitality and participation.

Lighting should be adequate, since much worship may be led from this spot, and it may be necessary to provide floor outlets for microphones. Displays of flowers or potted plants, as well as candlestands, will be located in this area. Sufficient room must be allowed as well for such seasonal items as an Advent wreath, Christmas decorations or trees, Easter flowers, and the paschal (Easter) candle. It is important that this space be large enough so it will never seem crowded.

Arrangement of Space

Finally, we need to look at the way these three centers and spaces relate to congregational space. Visibility and audibility from all three are essential. For the pulpit, sight lines are especially important. It is exceedingly difficult to preach to those on one's far left and right (as in the 180° arc of a circle). The preacher is forced to turn constantly in order to see and be seen by people at the extremities. It is better to preach to an arc no greater than 135 degrees, the majority of the congregation being within the 90 degree angle (see Fig. 6).

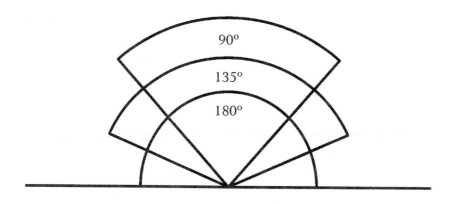

Figure 6

Such arrangements facilitate the best eye contact possible. In some recent buildings, the tendency has been to pull the pulpit back from the edge of congregational space in order to decrease the angle. Occasionally this places the pulpit behind or to one side of the altar-table, often on the main axis. In the New England meetinghouse, designed for preaching, the pulpit was always against the wall, thus decreasing the angle as much as possible. Similar locations have much to commend themselves today.

If there are balconies or galleries, further problems arise. Usually this means the pulpit must be rather elevated so the preacher can see all those to whom the sermon is addressed. But it should not be elevated any higher than is necessary to enable those in the balcony to see the face and hands of the preacher.

Care is required in locating choir space so the preacher's back is not turned to this important segment of the congregation. It should not be necessary for the choir to move before the sermon, as sometimes happens.

Much of what we have said about the location of the pulpit applies also to the presider's chair. The narrower the angle of the vision, the better the eye contact. This usually suggests placing the presider's chair against the rear wall. By contrast, altar-table space needs to be close to the congregation; hence, accessibility and proximity are important considerations.

The service of the Word is not the only type of worship the church must serve. We are not building an auditorium simply for hearing, but a place in which sacraments are celebrated. This means that every church building is a compromise between space most suitable for the sacraments and space most appropriate for the service of the Word. Inevitably, this means compromise. One congregation actually built two spaces — one for the service of the Word and another for the service of the Lord's Table; the people move from one space to the other. But most congregations must use the same space for both.

For preaching space, the essential image is a straight horizontal line between speaker and hearer. We can picture such space as having a horizontal axis, ranging along the extent of the speaker's voice:

Figure 7

For the sacraments, on the other hand, our image is that of a vertical line, centered on the altar-table or on the baptismal font or pool. People gather in concentric fashion about the celebrant, whose reach is only that of a human arm. Thus the eucharistic gathering may kneel or stand on three or four sides of the altar-table, and the baptismal party may surround the water. The celebrant forms a vertical axis at the center of a concentric circle.

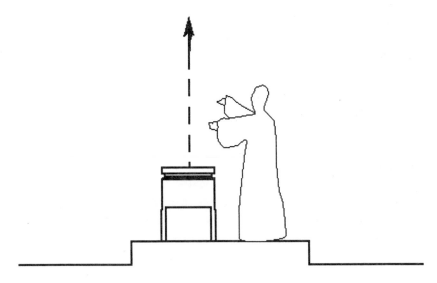

Figure 8

How do we reconcile these two types of buildings? It is not easily done, and every church is a compromise between a horizontal axis and a vertical one essentially, between pulpit and altar-table. Each congregation must decide the relative values of each type of space and find the most feasible compromise possible, so that preaching can be clearly seen and heard and yet people can feel gathered about the altar-table. Each building will be less than perfect for a single type of worship but we can hope for as good a solution as possible when all types of services are considered.

THREE

A PLACE FOR THE LORD'S SUPPER

When we turn to the Christian sacraments, we encounter some architectural requirements quite different from those for the service of the Word. Different concepts of space are necessary for Christian worship that centers in those sacred actions we call sacraments or ordinances. A few general characteristics of space used for these forms of worship should be explored before we discuss the Lord's Supper itself.

Various denominations celebrate the Lord's Supper in different ways; divergences take place even within a single church. Beneath this diversity, however, is an underlying similarity of action, derived from the same biblical foundations. Thus it is possible to analyze at the same time what is done in the Roman Catholic Mass and at the Baptist ordinance of the Lord's Supper.

The most desirable architectural setting and furnishings for this service have become remarkably similar in recent years, whatever the denomination concerned. We shall spell out the general spaces and furnishings considered most appropriate, while mentioning the special requirements of individual denominations.

Sacraments in General

Not all Christian bodies use the term *sacrament*, nor is there agreement on how many services this particular term applies to. For many Christians, the term *ordinance* is used for baptism and the Lord's Supper; *ordinance* also may apply to other services such as Christian marriage and funerals. Roman Catholicism counts seven sacraments: baptism, confirmation, eucharist, ordination, matrimony, reconciliation, and anointing of the sick. For most Protestants, *sacrament* applies only to baptism and the Lord's Supper, but we shall use the term here in the broadest sense. Much of this section applies also to the various ordinances that are no longer reckoned as sacraments but have similar characteristics, such as Christian burial.

These disparate forms of worship have common elements in that they focus on actions and objects rather than on words. Whereas the focus of the service of the Word is on seeing and hearing, the focus of sacramental worship is on action: Persons give themselves to each other through vows and rings, persons are washed with water, bread is broken, we bid farewell to a body. Each of these services uses words, but the real center of each is meaningful action performed in the midst of a worshiping community. In this action, the community experiences the presence of God in its midst.

In this sense, sacraments are sign-acts. God is experienced as using designated actions as a means of self-giving. These actions are thus effective signs; they accomplish what they signify. Baptism not only portrays cleansing but establishes a new relationship in which the baptized are related to God and to one another as forgiven people. In giving themselves to each other in the marriage service, two persons create a new reality, a Christian marriage.

As effective signs, the sacraments relate to the experience of the whole community. *We define sacraments as actions in which the whole Christian community experiences the present work of the Risen Christ.* These actions have a history in the community, functioning throughout time. They also have a universality as events in which the Christian community experiences the present action of the Risen Christ. They are communal experiences, and they relate each local community to all other Christian communities throughout space and time.

There are certain clear architectural implications to sacramental worship. Actions are central in experiencing Christ's present activity in the sacraments. Christ is acting through his ministers, but the actions are performed by humans; this means that the scale is always that of the human body—that is, a height of around six feet and a roughly equal armspread. The human body determines the size of baptismal fonts and pools, of altar-tables, of caskets, of everything to do with the sacraments. If, in a theological sense, the sacraments reflect the human side of God and God's concern for relating to us, this is equally so in the architectural sense, in that everything is scaled to human dimensions. Thus an altar-table is not an architectural monument or a spatial focal point but a furnishing scaled to the human who uses it.

If the scale of the human body is primary, then we must realize certain things about how the human body acts. Most of the sacraments involve a reaching out of the arms and hands of those who preside: to give bread and wine; to pour, sprinkle, or dip in water; to unite the hands of two persons. Whereas the human voice can project several hundred feet by natural means and be extended much farther artificially, there is no similar extension of the arm. People must come to the ministering person; arms cannot be stretched. At the heart of sacramental actions, then, is a gathering about, a coming within arm's reach—for individuals, if not for the whole community. One cannot anoint a person at a distance; one cannot lay on hands by remote control. So we are dealing with concepts of space quite different from those implied by the service of the Word.

Visibility, proximity, and accessibility are prime concerns in ordering space for sacramental worship. The entire community needs to be able to see the actions of those who preside. Breaking the bread is a meaningful act only when visible. We gather as witnesses when two persons give themselves to each other in marriage. Participating in the formation of new Christians through baptism calls for all to be able to see and hear water splash, trickle, or cascade into the font or pool, for salvation is portrayed by the feel of water against skin. The whole congregation participates in this act, and the people must be close enough to see and hear what happens.

Proximity to any human action makes it more personal. People attend political rallies to approach candidates in person, giving them a reality they lack in the media. Proximity makes participation more direct, intimate, and real. Thus the intensity of any experience is likely to be directly influenced by our proximity to the action. All our senses are affected by proximity; the closer we are to the action, the more it is a part of our being.

Long tunnel-like churches are the antithesis of proximity. Balconies are likewise problematic, especially when a community gathers at the altar-table. Time lost climbing stairs and walking down aisles almost limit churches with large balconies to preaching rather than celebration of the sacraments.

Accessibility is essential. The congregation must come within arm's reach of those ministering the bread and cup, without obstructions such as stairs or oncoming people. Unfortunately, the logistics in many churches require ingenuity on the part of worshipers because of the building's poor design.

The paradigm of a sacramental church (which ought not be followed literally in actual practice) is basically concentric space that is, a community gathered about a font or an altar-table, where someone reaches out to minister. The axis is vertical, reaching from the floor up through the particular liturgical center that is the focus of the action. Obviously, compromise is necessary, since a church also functions for services of the Word. Since the sacraments are primarily actions that relate to our senses, the degree of our participation is largely determined by the shape of the space in which we celebrate these sacraments.

Actions are often more ambiguous than words, so the sacraments are multivalent, conveying many messages. Both cleansing and incorporation are experienced in baptism, but the relative intensity of either may be shaped by the design of space and furnishings. Since there are many different meanings in each sacrament, some spaces favor one particular aspect of a sacrament but neglect other equally vital aspects. Eucharistic fellowship may be suggested by one use of space, awe and mystery by another. Not only must we balance the service of the Word with sacramental worship, we must also balance the different aspects of each sacrament in providing optimum space for its many dimensions of meaning.

The Lord's Supper

We must ask ourselves, then, just what various meanings Christians experience in each sacrament, beginning with the Lord's Supper. Different practices and meanings for the Lord's Supper predominate in various traditions. Even the names vary, yet all stem from the actions of Jesus at the last supper, and much of the subsequent history is common. So we can make many generalizations and mention only a few specific needs.

The Last Supper was a domestic liturgy, celebrated in a private home. And that remains the heart of it even today: a ritual meal based on actions associated with eating and drinking. Such a meal for us today implies two spaces in a private home: a kitchen for preparing food and a dining room for serving it. Both are rather small intimate spaces focused on the domestic actions of dining—preparation, blessing, serving, eating and drinking. The public spaces of a church magnify the scale greatly because a larger number of people are eating and drinking, although not much more space is necessary for preparation, blessing, or serving. It is helpful to bear in mind the analogies between domestic dining and a public celebration of the Lord's Supper.

Just as in the family situation, some actions, such as preparing the food and drink or serving them, are utilitarian. Other aspects of the meal—conversation, the blessing, eating and drinking together are far more than utilitarian for they are an integral part of family life or the association of friends. Even in such a situation, roles begin to develop; someone usually makes the salad, another takes care of the tea or coffee. Ritual acts soon develop as one person brings in the turkey, another carves the roast or serves the plates. Even a couple dining alone usually have arrived at distinct roles and rituals.

The analogy of a domestic meal is also helpful for understanding what goes on at the Lord's Supper in terms of space and furnishings. Primarily, we shall treat actions, since these are common to the different churches. And what we do in common calls for remarkably similar spaces.

The first action in any meal involves preparation; the Lord's Supper is no different. Some of this work occurs in the private space of the sacristy, where there is counter space and running water so that the communion vessels can be cleansed and prepared. The wine or grape juice will be poured from commercial bottles into flagons, decanters, or individual glasses at this point, since there is nothing edifying about these actions. The bread or wafers will be unwrapped and placed on a suitable ciborium, plate, basket, or paten.

The public acts of preparation involve presenting these items at the altar-table or uncovering them, if already in place. The wine or grape juice may need to be poured into chalices. The bread will need to be placed so it can be handled and broken at the right time. These are utilitarian acts to which time has given meaning, and we must make spatial provision so that meaning can be fully expressed.

The presentation of the bread and wine is both a practical act and an ethical statement. In the early church the communicants brought bread and wine as they were financially able. Other gifts, such as oil, cheese, and olives might also be presented. From the bread and wine presented, the deacons chose a small portion for the Lord's Supper; the rest of the gifts went to feed the poor. Thus the gathered assembly met the Lord both in the supper and by ministering to the world through the offerings. The modern church does the same, if less graphically, in the offering of bread and wine and money to minister to the world.

In many churches, the bread and wine are brought by representatives of the people to the Lord's Table with the other gifts. This necessitates a small table near the chief entrance to the congregational space. The bread and wine remain there until carried forward in the offertory procession. We also offer money, so a place must be provided for the offering plates or baskets after they are filled with gifts for the world: a small table or shelf is necessary somewhere near the altar-table.

As the bread and wine are prepared after being brought to the altar-table, it may be the custom for the presider to wash his or her hands in a small bowl while standing at one end of the altar-table. This demands a bowl, pitcher, and towel and a place to put them after the washing. The wine may be poured into chalices together with a bit of water, leaving empty decanters or flagons to be disposed of. All these items belong not on the altar-table but on a small table or shelf nearby. When the preparation is completed, only the service book and the bread and wine in their appropriate serving vessels remain on the altar-table. Offerings of money and empty vessels have been relegated to the small table or shelf. The altar-table is no longer the kitchen counter of preparation, but the dining table at the center of a banquet.

The next action before meals in Christian families is the giving of thanks, and this is one of the most important actions of the Lord's Supper. In this act — the eucharistic prayer — we proclaim the faith that makes us one by reciting what God has done for us already and asking God to act in our midst here and now and in future events. The chief medium is words, just as in the table blessing at home, but far more is at stake. By dialogue and sung responses, the congregation shares in this joint act of lifting up of hearts. Frequently the congregation stands for the entire prayer as does the person presiding. There is mutual participation even though the presider does most of the speaking. This, of course, means that the person presiding must be visible and audible to all those with whom he or she is praying.

The presider, facing the congregation, prays not only with the lips but with the arms, hands, the entire body. The prayer is full of expressive gestures that may include raising the arms to God, gesturing toward the congregation, touching the bread and cup. These actions demand sufficient open space so the presider can have room for the full human armspread behind the altar-table — six feet of unimpeded vertical and horizontal space. Nothing visual should compete with the presider in this approximately thirty-six square-foot (6 feet high by 6 feet wide) vertical plane behind the altar-table. The presider's silhouette should not be lost in a background of sculpture, murals, or stained glass or suffer from competition with plants or flower arrangements. The action of presiding at this prayer is essential, and the building should frame it rather than obscure it. The worst possibility is the glare of light from a large window behind and at the level of the presider. On sunny days, it can be painful to watch the action of this prayer.

At any meal, it is necessary to serve the food. The Breaking of Bread is one of the oldest names for this service. The bread needs to be broken because "we, who are many, are one body, for we all partake of the one loaf. The bread which we break is a sharing in the body of Christ"— a utilitarian act, to be sure, but one with profound meaning. The loaf must be broken so that all may share in it. With some methods, it may be necessary for several persons to assist the presider in breaking the bread, but the initial breaking is most easily and eloquently done at the altar-table, facing the congregation.

The next action does require considerable provision. The logistics of serving food and drink to even a few score people, let alone hundreds or thousands, all within ten or fifteen minutes, is no mean endeavor. This requires well-planned movement space for bringing the people to the bread and cup, or these to the people. Well-designed altar-table space is needed so the ministers of the Eucharist can move immediately to those who have not yet been served and can replenish the bread and wine. And congregational space must be planned so that people can come and go unimpeded by obstacles.

The crucial action in serving is that of giving the body and blood of Christ through the bread and wine. For the giving of so great a gift, this part of the service must not appear rushed or awkward, yet it should not seem unduly prolonged. This necessitates a communion rail or a place to kneel so that at least a tenth of those present can kneel at the same time. Or if communion is received standing, there must be sufficient communion stations, with access to each, so communicants do not return in the face of those yet unserved. Even pew communion can pose problems for distributing the elements to all parts of the congregation in a short time. Above all, the act of giving communion will show how carefully the building has been planned for the Lord's Supper.

These are the basic actions of the Lord's Supper. Others, such as passing the peace, putting the altar-table in order, disposing of the remaining bread and wine, making announcements, and the dismissal and departure of the congregation, do not seem to necessitate special provision of space.

Furnishings and Spaces

How do we best provide for those actions common to almost all celebrations of the Lord's Supper? We shall address the practice of most Protestant traditions, Anglicans, and western (Latin) rite Roman Catholics. The spatial demands for Orthodox, Oriental, and eastern-rite Roman Catholic worship are so distinctive they will not be discussed here.

The altar-table is the center of all these actions. The bread and wine are prepared here, the prayer takes place here, the bread is broken here, and from this place the bread and wine are taken to be given. These actual uses are primary and take precedence over the altar-table as a symbol or as the architectural focus of the building. It is meant to be used, not to symbolize or be admired.

The altar-table, though prominent in location, is not an immense item. The scale is the human who presides at it, so the length should not be more than five or six feet and the width half that. It is the height that is crucial. The kitchen counter, where one stands to work, is our model at this point, not the dining table. The altar-table should be thirty-nine or forty inches high. In many Protestant churches it is too low for practical use. Since the presider's hands need to be free, the service book must rest on the altar-table, and the distance from the eyes to the book makes reading it extremely difficult. Only in those churches where the congregation and presider actually sit around the altar-table is the thirty-inch dining-table height appropriate. Scale, then, is our first concern.

Form is our second concern. Whereas altar-tables in the past were often solid, suggesting a casket, a table-like shape is now preferred by many Roman Catholics and most Protestants. The emphasis, in our time, is focused on the meal aspects of the service, and the table form suggests this most strongly. It is possible also to suggest the aspect of sacrifice with a compact table made of substantial material. Since ordinary tables differ in their support from a single pedestal to five legs or even more, there is considerable latitude for design possibilities as long as the top is flat and of sufficient size and height. Experience has shown that round or oval tops do not function well, since it is difficult for the presider to stand in such a way that the body relates to the table's full length.

The material also can vary — usually wood, metal, or stone — but in any case, it should be of fine material and made with care. The use of plastics such as Lucite or plexiglass has intrigued designers, but the results usually have been unsatisfactory because the material does not seem substantial. Stone such as granite, marble, or slate provides enormous possibilities and the variety of woods an even greater selection.

Too frequently in the past, the altar-table was an architectural *tour de force* which dominated the congregation rather than ministered to it. Yet massive size and ornate decoration do not reflect the purpose of an altar-table. If it is conceived of in terms of ministry (i.e., use), rather than as a spectacle (i.e., visual impact), then most of these problems resolve themselves. A ministerial altar-table will be congruent with the community it serves and those who serve at it.

The location of the altar-table is as significant as its design. Where it and the space around it are situated will largely determine how the altar-table functions. First and foremost, it should be free-standing so that those using it can stand behind it, facing the congregation. This is now mandatory in some denominations and strongly advised in others. All the recent reforms in worship presuppose that the presider celebrates facing the congregation across the altar-table. Once one has done so, it is hard, if not impossible, to return to a position with one's back to the congregation. The sense of the family of God gathered about the altar-table is too strong an image to make any other position tolerable.

There is no particular need for the altar-table to be placed directly on the horizontal axis of the church. Symmetry is not particularly holy and some of the best recent churches have placed the altar-table off-center, in dynamic relationship with the pulpit, font, presider's chair, or a large cross. An off-center location actually may call more attention to the altar-table or improve its relation to congregational space.

There must be nothing behind the altar-table for a distance of at least four feet. Even more space is desirable for the movement of clergy in preaching robes or vestments. A generous amount of space is necessary at the ends of the altar-table, especially in traditions where the presider's hands are washed. Space before the altar-table is essential for various actions such as the greetings and the dismissal. In some traditions, the approach of clergy to the altar-table involves considerable ceremonial, which makes this space even more important. The altar-table, then, must be free-standing in a generous amount of space so that approach to it is not obstructed from any side.

In some cases, the space about the altar-table will need to be elevated by a single step so as to make the actions there visible to the whole congregation. The step should be well away from the altar-table itself so there is no danger that those who minister at it will accidentally step off. In general, the whole front portion of the church should be elevated just enough so that all that happens there is visible from the back, even by short people. But no more than a single step should distinguish the altar-table space, and even this may not be necessary if the whole area is sufficiently elevated.

Usually it is desirable to have floor candlestands, perhaps two or three at each end of the altar-table. The reformed services of our time make it advisable to keep the top of the altar-table clear of such things as candles, crosses, offering plates, flowers, Bibles, and anything not directly used in the Lord's Supper. This helps make all actions fully visible. The altar-table should hold only service books and the communion vessels.

Floor candlestands may need to be designed and made locally. They function best when they are the same height or slightly taller than the altar-table and each holds a single large candle. Today there is a general tendency to avoid brass in favor of wood, or metal painted black or the color of the church interior. The candlestands should be taken into consideration when planning the space about the altar-table.

At different seasons and feasts, the altar-table may be covered with cloth hangings. By color, texture, and design, these communicate the nature of the season or festival being celebrated. An altar frontal that covers the whole front of the altar-table may be used, but it should be designed by a professional artist and carefully made of quality materials for it will be the most conspicuous work of art in the entire building. Such a display is never necessary, and for most denominations, a simple white linen cloth the width of the top and dropping slightly over the ends is sufficient. This serves as a tablecloth and is primarily functional rather than symbolic.

In some denominations there are special requirements for altar-table space. In many of the Reformed and some Free Church traditions, seats are placed behind the altar-table for elders or deacons, who assist in distributing the bread and wine and may even proclaim the eucharistic prayer. In some churches these people occupy the first row of pews.

In an older Reformed pattern rarely seen in this country, although prevalent in the Netherlands, communicants sit about tables to receive communion. In early nineteenth-century Presbyterian churches in this country, a long table might be fixed in front of the first pew and a movable bench placed opposite it so as to accommodate communicants on both sides. The minister sat at one end and the bread and wine were passed the length of the table. Sometimes portable tables and benches were set up across the front of the church or even down the central aisle when the Lord's Sup-

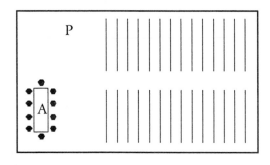

Figure 9

per was celebrated. A permanent arrangement can be seen in Washington Park United Church of Christ in Denver, Colorado, where chairs are arranged around a large table at one side of the front of the church (see Fig. 9).

A minor furnishing mentioned — a small table or shelf near the altar-table — receives the empty communion vessels; the bowl, pitcher, and towel for washing hands; and the offering plates. One should experiment to discover how large a surface is needed; often a lower shelf is necessary for the offering plates. If the font is located at the front of the church, the small table or shelf probably will be used at times to hold a pitcher and towels. In that case, it may be wise to have it convenient to both font and altar-table. It certainly should not be distant from the altar-table, since it will be used whenever the Lord's Supper is celebrated.

Another minor furnishing is a small table at the entrance of the church for the bread and wine prior to the offering procession. It is often moved aside after that point in the service, so it certainly should be movable. In some cases it may be wise to allow increased space around this table by shortening the pews near it so movement space is not clogged. Otherwise, experience has shown that people have a tendency to bump into it, a most unfortunate accident when it is laden with bread and wine. Both these small tables or shelves are purely functional and should not be prominent, but only large enough to hold what is necessary. If incense is used during the service, an unobtrusive stand should be provided on which to hang the thurible.

Space for the fourth of the main actions at the Lord's Supper, the giving of the bread and wine, is very important. There are three common ways to receive communion: in the pews by passing the bread and glasses, standing at communion stations, and kneeling at communion rails. In a fourth, as we have mentioned, the people sit about a table.

The requirements for pew communion are simple: chiefly little racks on the back of pews for the glasses, eliminating the need to collect them during the service. It may be convenient to place markers on pew ends so each usher knows where to begin passing the elements. Communion stations primarily involve movement space. Persons ministering the bread and cup can stand at the head of any aisle. This is also possible, though awkward, in balconies. People should have sufficient space to approach the communion station without crowding as they go from the person ministering the bread to the one with the cup. It is a challenge to plan movement space and congregational space so that the recirculating may be done without direct confrontation of people going in the opposite direction. The service will go much more smoothly if people can approach the communion stations by one or more aisles and return by others. There is no need for tables at communion stations. The bread and wine can be replenished by assistants, making it clear that all eat and drink from one altar-table.

The requirements for receiving communion in a kneeling position are more complicated. Communion rails are not a necessity. They were introduced, in part, to prevent dogs from coming near the altar-table—one problem we do not have today! (Bangor Cathedral in Wales still has a set of dog tongs used to remove unruly dogs.) Rails are helpful in kneeling, but other people can support infirm or pregnant persons. Communion rails should never appear as a barrier or wall about the altar-table. Occasionally they are made to be removable and placed in slots in the floor only when needed. In all cases they should be as open as possible. Where the wine is served in small glasses, it may be a convenience to have holes in the top of the rail where the glasses may be placed, avoiding the need for an additional person to collect them during the service.

Far more important than the rail is a step on which to kneel. This should be raised and padded. Frequently, cushions of needlepoint made by members of the congregation give an opportunity for an offering of local time and talent.

Increasingly, the kneeling step and communion rails (if any) surround the altar-table on three sides instead of running straight across the front of the church. This gives a greater sense of gathering about the altar-table as the family of God, and also accommodates many more people, measurably lessening the time spent waiting in line. Two things are important for the space within the rails. It should be wide enough that two persons dressed in clergy robes may pass without crowding or colliding with pulpit, font, or altar-table. There is considerable movement by several persons in this space during communion. The area in which the ministers of communion walk should be no higher than the step on which people kneel and preferably the same height as the floor beyond the kneeling step. It is very awkward to distribute communion when the server is standing on a level higher than that on which people are kneeling. In some cases, they may receive the elements at communion stations, then kneel at will at the rail for a few moments of prayer.

In some traditions, communion rails have important functions other than at the Lord's Supper. They are used for altar prayers at a time when people are invited to come forward to pray; the communion rail, in these instances, is often referred to as "the altar." It may also be used for "altar call," when people are invited to come forward to dedicate or rededicate their lives. On Ash Wednesday, people may kneel at the rail while they receive ashes on their foreheads, and the same rail may be used during healing services and confirmations.

Two points should be made in ending our discussion of space and furnishings for the Lord's Supper. Only one altar-table should be in the chief space used for worship. Others may appear in a weekday, or eucharistic, chapel or another distinctly separate space. But the principle of only one altar-table to a church is now affirmed by the major denominations as a symbol of the unity of the body of Christ. The body of Christ is one, and a single altar-table best manifests this.

There ought to be a separate and distinct place for the tabernacle in Roman and Anglo-Catholic churches. Recent reforms have forbidden its presence on the altar-table and encourage giving it a place of honor in a separate place, such as a chapel. Extraliturgical devotions should not compete with the celebration of the Eucharist. When the tabernacle is directly behind the altar-table, the presider must celebrate with his or her back to it, and it competes visually with the Mass. The actions at the altar-table are primary, and a neutral background helps the people concentrate on what is done there. Nothing should distract attention from the actions of the Christian community as it gathers to celebrate the Lord's Supper.

Four

A PLACE FOR BAPTISM

The Christian Church is not primarily an organization or an institution, but a community of those baptized into the death and resurrection of Jesus Christ. The Church rests on the promises of God proclaimed in baptism and allows those promises to lead it forward into God's future. In recent decades, a renewed understanding of our identity as Church has been reflected in a reformation of Christian initiation, a reformation which has involved not only the rites of baptism but the whole framework on which it rests.

Our search for a revitalized understanding of the nature of Christian initiation has led us back to the rich scriptural imagery surrounding baptism. Returning to the narratives of the Old Testament in which the chosen people of God are saved through the waters of the flood (Gen. 6 8) and the parting of the Red Sea (Exod. 14), we have discovered the role water has played in God's mighty saving deeds. The New Testament discourses on baptism add further layers of meaning to the event of Christian initiation. The baptized are cleansed from sin and born anew, buried with Christ, raised with Christ, and enlivened by the Holy Spirit. Each of the new rites of Christian initiation reflects, in one way or another, this recovery of biblical imagery and of a theology rooted in Scripture.

The witness of Scripture also has helped us appreciate the myriad ways in which God uses people, places, and things in reaching out to human beings with the offer of abundant life. This idea that God conveys divine realities by means of physical substances is broadly referred to as *sacramentality* and has had a profound impact on recent baptismal theology and practices. The new rites take seriously the roles of persons who witness to the truth of the gospel, the places where the Christian community gathers, and the water and human gestures which testify to the generous and reconciling love of God.

Other changes rest on renewed interest in the history of Christian initiation. As heirs to more than a century of liturgical scholarship, we have been able to reach back into the Christian past to hear the witness of the church- especially the early church on the nature of baptism. In so doing, we have found clear evidence of a process of initiation which originally was complete in one event, an event consisting of a water bath, the laying on of hands by the bishop, and Holy Communion.

We have discovered that, by a series of historical accidents and theological misunderstandings, a breakdown in the unity of Christian initiation took place during successive centuries. Water baptism by itself began to be seen as somehow incomplete, requiring a later "confirmation" to ratify it. In virtually all denominations, the most recent generation of services of Christian initiation mark a return to the practice of the heroic age of the church, declaring that in baptism one is made a member of the body of Christ fully and unconditionally.

Contemporary theological reflection also has been an important factor in the reformation of the rites of Christian initiation. Study in the area of ecclesiology, the theology of the nature of the church, has been especially fruitful and has had a remarkable impact on the theology and practice of baptism. We have begun to take seriously the idea that each new Christian brings unique gifts and graces to the Church's mission in the world. This means that whenever an individual is incorporated, by water and the Holy Spirit, within the body of Christ, it is a matter of crucial importance to the Church as a whole.

For this reason, all the new services of Christian initiation have insisted that baptism is a public event, an act of the Church gathered in a particular time and place for worship on the Lord's Day. The Christian community is an active participant in the baptism of each individual, and the notion of 'private baptism' has begun to be seen as a contradiction in terms. In baptism, the congregation assumes responsibility for the Christian nurture of the baptized, prays for the continuing action of the Holy Spirit in their lives, and welcomes them as full members of the body of Christ.

Each of these recent developments has contributed to a dramatic change in the theology of Christian initiation, in the shape of the rites of Christian initiation, and in baptismal practice. A return to a theology of baptism based upon biblical norms has given the language of the rites a renewed depth and richness. A return to the practice of Christian initiation as based on sound historical research has reestablished that practice as an action of the gathered community. A return to a fuller sense of God's use of the material in human life has occasioned a renewed appreciation of the ritual and symbolic power of the rites of Christian initiation. All these changes have serious implications for the architectural environment of Christian baptism.

Baptismal Space

In terms of church architecture, there are really only two essential components for the rites of Christian initiation: a container for water and a place to put that container. The challenge for those who build and renovate, however, is to create out of these simple components a setting within which the words and actions of baptism can communicate to the whole Christian community. We strive to create a place where the words can speak of forgiveness, the water can speak of abundant life and cleansing, and the human gesture can speak of welcome.

The location of baptismal space has the power to say a great deal about the role of baptism in the life of the community. It can proclaim that Christian initiation lies either at the center of Christian existence, or at its periphery. It can proclaim that Christian initiation is either a private transaction between God and the individual, or a matter of profound significance to the whole Christian community. It can say that Christian initiation is either a mysterious and closely-guarded ritual, or an open and generous invitation to new life.

Unfortunately, over the past several decades the location of baptismal space has generally been seen as a matter of indifference, to be dictated simply by considerations of convenience or design. More recently, however, we have begun to realize that one of the most important elements in the renewal of Christian initiation is a rethinking of the space in which baptism takes place.

Whatever location is ultimately chosen for the baptismal font or pool, the first consideration is to surround it with a sufficient amount of open space. The presider, parents of the candidates, godparents or sponsors, and the candidates themselves all need to be gathered immediately around the font or pool in order to participate in the rites of Christian initiation. As congregations move to the celebration of "baptismal festivals" at which many candidates are baptized, the space will need to accommodate still larger numbers of people. In some traditions, representatives from the governing body of the community are also present. Occasionally, and especially in the case of the baptism of infants, the children in the congregation may be asked to come to the baptismal space so that they might share more fully in the event of making new Christians, and perhaps even voice their own prayers for the candidates.

Because the most recent generation of baptismal services in the mainline denominations proclaim that Christian initiation is a public act, with the gathered community taking an active and essential role, the second general requirement for the location of baptismal space is that it be where the whole congregation can see and hear the action. This return to the idea that baptism is an act of the church dictates that the place in which it occurs not be hidden away in a side chapel or placed in an alcove or transept. The location chosen must clearly testify that the making of new Christians is not a matter of private concern only, but the concern of the whole body of Christ. For this reason, the acoustics of the space need careful consideration.

As the Church has reflected upon the ways in which the location of baptismal space speaks to the community, two alternatives for the placement of the baptismal font or pool have particularly begun to recommend themselves. The first of these is near the entrance of the church, either within the main worship space or in the gathering space. This location proclaims to all that it is through the waters of baptism that one enters the community of faith and becomes a member of the body of Christ. Each individual coming into or leaving the church building encounters the witness of the water of forgiveness and regeneration, and in so doing confronts anew the meaning of baptism in his or her own life.

There are certain disadvantages to this location, however. First, it is less accessible to the community during the actual celebrations of baptism. In order for members of the congregation to see the action at the font or pool, they must either leave their seats and gather in the baptismal space or stand and turn around to face the rear. For the latter option, pews must be set wider apart to avoid bumped knees and shins. In many small congregations, either standing in the congregational space or gathering in the baptismal space are possible options. But in larger congregations, this location presents sufficient difficulties to make it a less-than-perfect solution. In some situations a font can be made moveable, standing normally at the entrance to the church but transferred to a more central location for the celebration of a baptism. Some people object quite strenuously to this option, however, claiming that the font should be a stable architectural element, symbolizing in its unchanging position the steadfastness of the promises of God ratified in Baptism.

The second option is to place the baptismal space in the same general area as the other liturgical centers, usually near the front or center of the worship space. In this arrangement, the grouped altar-table, pulpit, and font give a vivid visual proclamation of the nature of the Christian life, a life quickened by the gospel, born of water and the Holy Spirit, and nourished by the body and blood of Jesus Christ. Each time the congregation gathers for worship, whether or not a baptism is celebrated, attention is focused on the font, which testifies to the power of God at work in the baptized community.

There are also certain practical advantages to placing the font in this location. In most cases, a serious effort has been made to ensure that the pulpit and altar-table are accessible to the community, that every person present can see and hear the action taking place around them. This location participates in the success of this effort, allowing the action of baptism, every time it occurs, to unfold within full sight and hearing of the whole community. The acoustics in this situation are also likely to be good as well.

Clearly, the question of the location of the baptismal space cannot be practically separated from the question of the kind of vessel that will contain the water used. Many of the same shifts in our baptismal theology and practice that have dictated changes in baptismal space also have dictated changes in the baptismal font or pool. In addition, the space we provide will, to a large degree, be shaped around the sort of vessel we provide, and the vessel itself will be shaped by the space in which it is located.

Because we have come to a renewed understanding of the power of material creation to convey the self-giving of God, we have begun to be concerned over the ways in which that creation is used in the sacraments (cf. chap. 3). In baptism, the primary material used is water, and we have begun to focus on the ways water can best communicate forgiveness, rebirth, the work of the Holy Spirit, acceptance, and reconciling love. More and more, we have come to realize that in order to convey these things adequately, the water of baptism must be seen and heard by all members of the congregation.

This realization about the sacramental power of water also has begun to engender a profound transformation in the way we practice Christian initiation. Increasingly, we find that communities are moving to the use of larger quantities of water in order that the generosity of God's love might be made clear. Some communities which traditionally have sprinkled baptismal candidates with water have begun to immerse (submerse) or dip both infants and adults; in other places, the pouring of a substantial amount of water over the head of the candidate has become common. In either case, a larger-than-usual container for water must be considered.

The Baptismal Vessel

But for those who build and renovate church buildings, providing a font which both allows the water to speak clearly and enables baptism by pouring or immersion presents serious challenges. In most existing churches, the font is simply not large enough for the amount of water necessary to achieve either of these goals. And although many recent renovations have aimed at removing inadequate fonts, finding satisfactory substitutes has proved difficult. In addition, those who choose to retain a font (rather than installing a baptismal pool that would allow for the immersion of adults) find little help from the usual sources of information about church furnishings.

A font adequate to the needs of the Christian community and to the new services of Christian initiation must have two essential qualities. First, it should be a strong, well-designed form, a form which proclaims clearly and unequivocally that this is a container for water. Second, the font should be large enough to allow a sufficient amount of water to be used. Even if a particular congregation may not at present practice immersion of an infant, it should not bind its future practice by providing a font so small it prohibits such a method. A basin at least two feet in diameter is required, since babies usually are at least twenty inches long.

Securing a font with these qualities can tax the ingenuity of even the most creative of congregations. Few if any church-goods suppliers offer a font adequate to the needs of these newly revised services. Commercial fonts on the whole are poorly designed, with bowls too small by far for the quantities of water necessary. Sadly, even those congregations that look to the talents of design professionals will be faced with problems. Because the commercial houses have flooded American church buildings with inadequate fonts, the architect or designer who would like to create one sufficient for the needs of a community may have serious difficulty in finding a model.

Many congregations have managed to overcome these difficulties quite successfully. Some communities have found that photographs in such publications as *Environment and Art in Catholic Worship* (cf. chap. 10) have enabled them to describe their needs to an architect or designer with more confidence and accuracy. Others, especially those involved in renovation projects, have forged more innovative solutions. Often an object such as a washtub, a disk from a harrow, a wok, an inverted skylight, or the kind of bowl found in restaurant salad bars has been crafted and transformed into a font simply by adding a sturdy and well-designed base.

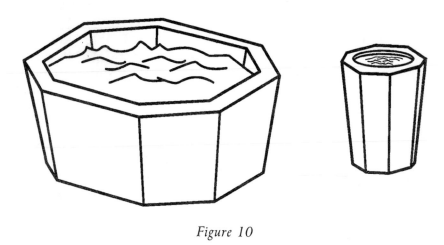

Figure 10

Congregations that wish to install a baptismal pool rather than a font have a bit more help available. Several companies manufacture such pools, and the experience of Baptist and Christian (Disciples of Christ) communities in their use and installation can be a valuable resource. The same general requirements for baptismal space and location apply to the pool as to the font. But because the baptismal pool is basically a hole in the floor, there is some difficulty in making it a dramatic visual image. A certain amount of design talent is required to give it the prominence it deserves.

Some practical details are associated with both the font and the pool, one of which is the matter of the water they contain. In some fonts and pools, the water is present all the time, whether an actual baptism is being celebrated or not, its presence continually testifying to the reconciling power of God. However, in order to keep the water from becoming stagnant, mechanical recirculation systems or chemical additives may be necessary. Recirculation has the added advantage of producing the sound of flowing water, which makes its own statement as it reverberates throughout the building. In cold climates, provision for heating the water may also be required.

In other cases, the water is added to the font or pool shortly before a baptism is to take place. If this is done during the service of baptism itself, as is recommended in the rites of some denominations, one or more attractive pitchers will be necessary. Whether the pool or font is left permanently filled or is filled just prior to the baptism, there is no reason for any cover to be placed upon it. The tradition of covers for fonts began in the Middle Ages to prevent water being stolen by those who believed it to possess magical powers. Since this is not a current problem, font covers would no longer seem to be a necessity. If safety is a concern with regard to baptismal pools at floor level, a transparent webbing can be placed just below the surface of the water to insure that a child cannot accidentally drown. The webbing can be removed when a baptism is to be celebrated.

Other Requirements

More and more often, the celebration of baptism requires a certain number of accessories, and for this reason a second practical necessity is a small table to be set up near the font or pool. On this table can be placed such items as pitchers, towels, a baptismal shell, oil for chrismation, and new garments and candles to be given to the candidates. This table need not be a permanent fixture of the baptismal space, but it should be well-designed and sturdy.

A final necessity in those churches that practice baptism by immersion or dipping is a changing room for the candidates and the presider. For the convenience and comfort of the participants, this room should be located adjacent to the baptismal space. In many churches the sacristy fulfills this need, but in any case, care must be taken to ensure that the flooring, both in the changing room and along the path toward it, cannot be damaged by dripping water.

One of the objects more and more commonly associated with baptism, as well as with other special services of the church, is the paschal (or Easter) candle, an ancient symbol of the light of Christ and of the Resurrection. This candle is large (at least 36 inches tall) and marked with the current year and symbols of Christ (see Fig. 11). For most of the year, this candle is placed near the font or baptismal pool and lighted whenever there is a baptism, as a sign of new life in the Risen Christ. Not only must sufficient space be allowed for the paschal candle near the font, but a substantial candlestand (4 feet tall) must be provided. In many churches this candle is stationed near the altar-table and pulpit from Easter until Ascension and, during a funeral, is placed at the head of the casket.

Another item of church furnishing related to baptism is the holy-water stoup. In many churches,

Figure 11   these small basins are located at the entrance to the worship space and filled with water that has been blessed. On entering the church, worshipers dip their fingers into this water, often marking themselves with the sign of the cross in thankful remembrance of their baptism. If holy-water stoups are a part of local tradition, they should be of generous proportion and demonstrate their connection to baptism by being of the same material and basic shape as the baptismal font, though smaller. In those churches which have placed the font at the entrance to the church, the holy-water stoup has been made redundant, and the water used as a reminder of baptism is taken from the baptismal font itself.

A final question to be considered is that of baptismal iconography. Although a number of images and symbols have become associated with Christian initiation over the centuries (such as the dove, the shell, the symbols of the Trinity), it is always the baptismal font or pool itself that is the primary sign of baptism. If it says clearly that it holds water and that baptism takes place in that water, it offers to the community the most profound possible image of the richness of baptism. Such a font needs no additional symbols applied to its surface. Sometimes a painting, a sculpture, or an example of fabric art can add beauty and warmth to the baptismal space, but if it is a representational (rather than abstract) piece, the subject matter should be related to the event of baptism itself.

There may be no more important single factor in the success or failure of the recent reforms in Christian initiation than the shape of the space in which they occur. A rite which proclaims that baptism is an event of consequence to the whole community cannot shout above a baptismal space which proclaims that it is a rarified moment between the individual and God. A service which speaks of the love of God made manifest in water cannot overcome a font which declares that water is unimportant. For better or worse, it is not only baptism that is shaped by the space we provide for it, but also the baptized community as a whole.

FIVE

A PLACE FOR THE
SERVICE OF MARRIAGE

If there is anything in the body of liturgical prose that is familiar to us, it is the language of the wedding service. For more than five hundred years, English-speaking Christians have been giving themselves to each other in marriage "for better for worse, for richer for poorer, in sickness and in health," and in the newest revisions of the marriage rites they continue to do so. But despite the conservatism of the latest generation of denominational resources, there are some major differences which need to be taken into account when designing or renovating a church building.

The most significant of these changes for the architectural setting is the reestablishment of the marriage rite as a full service of Christian worship. As in other kinds of worship, the community gathers, prayers are offered, Scripture read, a homily preached, and the Lord's Supper is sometimes celebrated. There is, of course, a special emphasis in the marriage service. We come into the presence of God to witness solemn public promises made by two people who are joining in marriage, to pray for God's blessing upon their life together, and to thank God for the witness of their love. The marriage of Christians, then, is not a fashion show or a flower show. It is not a photo or videotaping session, nor is it a showcase for the singing talents of family members. It is the worship of Almighty God, a thanksgiving celebration for the love of God manifested in the lives of two people.

In some small, stable, and particularly close-knit communities, we find the service of Christian marriage is often incorporated within the ordinary Sunday gathering. When a young man and woman have grown up in the congregation, have centered their lives among family and friends in Sunday school, youth groups, and at worship, it seems entirely natural and appropriate to celebrate their marriage on a Sunday morning when the whole community is gathered in prayer. Indeed, this may be the paradigm for the marriage of all Christians.

But most of us live in a less cohesive world. We find ourselves, at one and the same time, members of a variety of communities — home, church, neighborhood, school, work place, political party, to name just a few — all of which make social claims upon us. More and more often, those who gather for a wedding come together from a number of these communities and have little in common with one another beyond acquaintance with the bride or groom.

But despite their diversity, those who gather for the celebration of Christian marriage form — at least for a short time — a new community, united in love, happiness, and concern for the bride and groom. During the service itself the wedding guests are asked to unite even more closely as they join in certain acts of Christian worship with, and on behalf of, the couple. They will be asked to add their *Amen!* to the work God has begun in the lives of the couple and to pray that the marriage be a sign of the love of Christ for the world.

Space for the Marriage Service

Because of the special nature of the community that gathers for a marriage service, providing a suitable space presents particular challenges. Unlike those who come together for an ordinary Sunday service, some of these people will not have seen one another for many years. Others have never met before. Elderly or infirm relatives who rarely travel will have made a special effort to join in the celebration. As a result, the place where they come together must be designed to encourage and enable these individuals to forge, for this one occasion at least, a worshiping community. The gathering space must be gracious and hospitable, and it must invite conversation and interaction. It should be a place for human encounter, not just for "passing through." Each of these requirements for the gathering space has been noted earlier (cf. chap. 1), but they take on a special urgency in the case of Christian marriage.

Once the community has gathered, the service continues with a series of words and actions by which two people give themselves to each other in the presence of God and witnesses. Hands are joined and rings are exchanged, promises are given and prayer is offered. In all this, the gathered community is not simply a passive observer, but an active participant. Those present pledge to support the bride and groom in their life together, offer prayer on their behalf, then greet them for the first time as husband and wife. This emphasis on the participation of the community is one of the hallmarks of the new services of Christian marriage in all denominations.

Because of this emphasis on participation, and because the rite of Christian marriage is so eloquent, it is important that both the words and the action of the wedding service be given every opportunity to speak clearly to each member of the community present. In addition, the renewed understanding of the rite of Christian marriage as Christian worship has made certain important demands upon the building and the space within which the wedding takes place. Today we find that liturgical concerns are guiding decisions about the kind of space appropriate for Christian marriage rather than, as sometimes in the past, concern for social conventions or the convenience of florists and photographers.

Once the community has gathered and formed, the wedding party and those who will preside at the marriage assemble in the church. Just as there are many ways for the leaders in ordinary services of worship to assemble in the church, there are many ways for the wedding party to assemble. Most of the new rites simply say that the "persons to be married with their witnesses enter," or "assemble," or "gather," with no rubrical indication as to how this is to be accomplished. Sometimes the bride and groom simply greet their guests at the main door of the church and proceed with them to seats near the front of the worship space. The presider(s) then enter according to the custom of that particular community.

In some churches it is the practice for the presider(s), bride, groom, their attendants, family members, and those who will read lessons or lead in prayers, to enter together through a side door near the front of the church and take their places where they can be seen and heard by all present. For many couples today, entering together has proved an important symbol of the equality of bride and groom. The sacristy door is often the most convenient way for the members of the wedding party to enter the church, and in that case they and the presider(s) will gather in the sacristy shortly before the service is to begin. This is yet another argument for a sacristy of ample size, with a number of full-length mirrors (cf. chap. 3).

Perhaps the most familiar type of entrance is the bridal procession, in which the bride and her attendants enter together from the rear of the church (usually to rather triumphal music) and move to meet the groom, his attendants, and the presider(s) at the front. (Indeed, the phrase "to march down the aisle" has become a common synonym for marrying.) Architecturally, the tradition of the bridal procession has had a considerable impact on the shape of the church building, having been a major argument for the arrangement of congregational seating on either side of a central aisle.

Today we have begun to discover that the desire to accommodate a bridal procession does not absolutely necessitate providing a central aisle. In many cases the emphasis on the equality of bride and groom has transformed the bridal procession into two simultaneous processions—one for the bride, her family, and attendants, and another for the groom, his family, and attendants while the congregation sings an entrance hymn. Two side aisles are a more desirable option in this instance. (The custom of the wedding procession also can provide another strong argument for a narthex or gathering space of sufficient size to accomodate a wedding party waiting to proceed to the front of the worship space.

Any aisle — central, side, or other — that will accommodate a bridal procession must be a bit wider than that for the ordinary Sunday service (cf. chap. 1), since the fashion of bridal attire can dictate a skirt width of as much as five feet, and the bride's escort will take up more space still. In addition, more and more brides are requesting that both parents serve as escorts, which increases the necessary aisle width still further. These same requirements apply to doors through which the wedding party must pass.

Once the wedding party and presider(s) have entered the church, they usually gather in the space just in front of the first row of congregational seating. There the presider greets those present, describes the purpose for which they are gathered, and asks the bride and groom to declare publicly their intention to marry. In most of the new rites, the presider also asks the members of the congregation to affirm their willingness to support the man and woman in their life together. At this point the parents of the bride and groom may present them to be married, although in many of the newer wedding services this is strictly optional. Here a second architectural consideration comes into play. Many churches do not have sufficient space between the first row of pews and the chancel step or rail to accomodate these actions, which gives the whole procedure a cramped and uncomfortable feeling.

The very essence of these dialogues between presider and couple is that they are public. Because the congregation plays an important role in witnessing the vows and promising to support those who take them, it is especially important that all be able to see and hear the proceedings. The demands for adequate sight lines and acoustics and feeling of intimacy which apply to other gatherings of the Christian community certainly apply in the case of the service of Christian marriage.

After the greeting, exhortation, and exchange of declarations of intent, the service continues with the proclamation of the Word of God. This usually consists of prayer, Scripture readings, congregational responses in the form of a hymn, song, or psalm, and a homily or "charge to the couple." Once again, the architectural setting most appropriate to the service of the Word will work in favor of this portion of the marriage service. Readers may have entered with the wedding party, may come to the pulpit from their places in the congregation, or, especially in small weddings, may stand and read the lesson from their seats. Likewise, the homily may be delivered from the pulpit, from the aisle, or from the space just in front of the congregational seating.

The most conspicuous need peculiar to the wedding service at this point consists of seating for the members of the wedding party during the proclamation of the Word. Often the first row of congregational seating may be left vacant for this purpose, or portable seating can be arranged in a convenient place. It is possible that this seating for the members of the bridal party could be placed in the chancel area, but this would seem to be a less desirable option, encouraing congregational attention to be drawn to them rather than to the proclamation of the Word of God. Again, the area in front of the first row should be sufficiently spacious to allow for the provision of such seating.

The service continues with the marriage vows, during which the bride and groom make promises to each other and exchange rings or other tokens, and prayer is offered for their life together. For this part of the service, the wedding party usually moves into the space before the altar-table, which should be large enough to accommodate a considerable number of people. If this space is not sufficiently large, the attendants can remain in their seats while the bride, groom, best man, and maid or matron of honor enter the chancel with the presider(s).

During this portion of the service, prayers of thanksgiving and intercession are offered and the presider asks God to bless the marriage. If local tradition is to kneel for prayer, individual kneelers should be provided for the wedding party. Often a portable prayer desk (*prie-dieu*) is brought in for the bride and groom to kneel upon as they receive the nuptial blessing.

More and more often, the wedding service continues with the Lord's Supper, making it the first action in which bride and groom join as husband and wife. The members of the wedding party return to the seats they occupied for the service of the Word, and the celebrant prepares for the Lord's Supper. Often the bride and groom will act as offering bearers, carrying the bread and wine to the altar-table from a small table placed at the rear of the church. In every other respect the architectural requirements for the celebration of the Lord's Supper at a wedding are the same as for any other such celebration (cf. chap. 3). In any case, the Lord's Supper should never be a "spectator sport," and unless the congregation can and will participate fully, it should be transferred to another occasion rather than be staged as a service for the wedding party only.

Special Requirements

Many churches have a weekday, or eucharistic, chapel in addition to the main worship space (see chap. 8), and such a location is often an ideal setting for a smaller wedding. A chapel can provide the qualities of warmth and hospitality all weddings demand but which are difficult to achieve in a large space, especially when few people are gathered. If there is flexible seating in the chapel, it can be arranged to form aisles, a semicircle around the wedding party and presider, or any other configuration to support the action. In the main worship space, a small wedding may be held in a transept, or front pews can be screened off to form a more intimate space.

On occasion, a bride and her attendants will wish to prepare for the wedding at the church, and a room for that purpose is often provided. Such a dressing-room should have a dressing table, mirrors, and a source of running water and toilet facilities nearby. It should be located with easy access to the various places from which the bride may enter the church or chapel. Ideally, its placement should not require the wedding party to walk outside or through the body of the church before the service.

Although we have stressed that the wedding is not an occasion to showcase family talent, some congregations are willing to allow the couple a fairly free hand when it comes to the selection and performance of wedding music. Increasingly this has meant that traditional organ music is replaced by electronically enhanced and recorded music. This is another consideration in planning for sufficient electrical outlets in and around the chancel area. (c.f. ch. 7) Running extention cords to "octopus" plugs can be dangerous. Fire hazards may be created and liability may result from poor planning in this area.

A wedding is one of those occasions in which people from outside the community may be involved, and occasionally their presence has implications for the architectural setting. Florists are often less than respectful of the buildings they seek to decorate and need to be carefully supervised. One florist armed with a hammer and tacks can destroy a vast amount of woodwork and paint in a very short time. Floral displays should never obscure the primary symbols of the faith or be placed upon altar-table, font, or pulpit.

Photographers and video-tapers also may disrupt the service of Christian marriage or damage the place in which it occurs. In order to get "just the right effect," photographers have been known to use furnishings as camera mounts, or even climb onto the pulpit or altar-table. Each congregation should have a set of firm guidelines to define the roles of both photographers and florists. Such guidelines can avoid expensive repairs.

Finally, many congregations request that rice and confetti not be thrown at weddings held inside their church buildings. Both rice and confetti are difficult to clean up; the presence of rice on hard flooring can be a serious safety hazard; and confetti can bleed its color into porous surfaces and carpeting. Indeed, these reasons seem sufficient to restrict the use of either in and around the church building. In the interest of the ecology, birdseed is sometimes suggested as an acceptable alternative.

The understanding of the service of Christian marriage as a service of Christian worship is one of the most significant changes in the new generation of official denominational liturgical resources. Although the church building will sometimes be used for marriages that are not associated with Christian worship, each community has a responsibility to provide a setting within which the words and actions of the service of Christian marriage can speak clearly. Equally important to the rite of Christian marriage is the design of a space within which all the members of the congregation can function as participants in worship, not merely as passive observers, as they enter into a new relationship with the couple and promise them their support and encouragement.

Six

A PLACE FOR
CHRISTIAN FUNERALS

We have two questions to ask: What does the Christian community do as a community in the event of death? What kinds of space do these actions require?

We are talking about the death of a Christian. Many commercial establishments provide space for the burial rites of others (and for Christians, as well). But our concern here is for those members of a Christian community whose death is commemorated by the community in the church building.

The Christian Funeral

In many instances, it is now necessary to make a case for having the funeral of a Christian in the church building. So completely has modern commerce succeeded in secularizing our burial customs that it no longer can be taken for granted that Christians will be buried from the place where they worshiped, rather than from an alien commercial establishment. Yet there are signs of resistance to this form of secularization, of insistence that the church is where worship belongs in the event of the death of a Christian. There are several reasons for this.

Since one of the community's chief ministries is to surround the bereaved with a supportive presence, the church building itself provides a major element of that support with its familiar spaces and furnishings. A lifetime of joys and sorrows are associated with this place; it is fitting that a Christian life be commemorated among familiar people in a familiar place. The community cannot be its normal self in a strange location, and its message that friends are here to help is muted in unfamiliar surroundings.

The church should have control of the entire service. Lowest-common-denominator religious symbols in funeral directors' generic space lack the power of a group's own rich symbols. Frequently, funeral homes lack any symbols of the resurrection, since that might offend some people. The musical facilities rarely include a pipe organ; taped music is no substitute for live musicians, and usually its quality is deplorable. Frequently, a choir is possible in a church funeral; rarely, if ever, in a funeral home. The event should be controlled by the community of faith which gathers for the funeral, not by those who profit from it. Some denominations simply insist on this and have all funerals in their churches.

Nowhere in life is the ministry of the Christian community, as a community, more visible than in the event of death. This may be less apparent in new suburban churches where death is a rare and unexpected occurrence, but eventually it happens in all communities. And in these events, the Christian community ministers to the bereaved and deceased in a variety of ways. It unites in worship for the funeral but also continues its ministry in the weeks and years to come as the bereaved are reintegrated into its midst.

Our concern here is with one of these ministries, the service of Christian burial. The Christian community gathers to proclaim the power of God in the face of death. Death is the ultimate challenge to belief in the power and love of God, and the service of burial is the community's bold and defiant proclamation of its continuing trust in God. Every service of Christian burial focuses primarily on the promises of God declared in Scripture, and much of the service revolves around the reading and proclaiming of God's Word. In death as in life, the community gathers to hear what word there is from the Lord, and it hears of comfort and assurance. The Word that is proclaimed is the same as that heard each Sunday but now has a special urgency: Trust in God. There is a definite link between the place where this Word is proclaimed weekly throughout life, and the moment of death, when it is heard in a different context but in the same place among the same people. First of all, then, the community gathers to proclaim the power of God, even in the face of death.

The community gathers also to give thanks for the life that has been lived. It commemorates not life in general but a specific human life that has now ended. In this sense, it is a very personal type of service — not a generic form but one that focuses on what was distinctive about this particular life. When the community gathers to commemorate God's acts, whether in ancient history or for creating this particular life, it never fails to give thanks, sometimes in prayers and hymns addressed to God. Increasingly, the Lord's Supper is celebrated at funerals as a communal form of giving thanks for this specific life, in confidence that death is not the final victor but that God "gives us the victory through our Lord Jesus Christ" (1 Cor. 15:57).

A very important part of the service of Christian burial is simply the physical presence of a supportive community that surrounds the bereaved. Just being there when the need is greatest is more important than saying or doing anything in particular. Nor does this end with the funeral itself. It is a matter of being together in the other scenes of the death process at the home and at the graveyard. The custom of bringing in food for the family is a tangible expression of the importance of simply being present for the sake of those bereaved.

The service of Christian burial has another function — namely, that of commending the deceased to God's care. Just as in life the community unites in prayer for one another, so in death it gives thanks for the life that has been lived and commends the deceased to God's continuing care. This is largely an act of prayer.

Finally, there is the function of committing the body to the earth or sea. This is more than a purely utilitarian function, for it makes visible the separation of the deceased from the active life of the community. There can be serious dangers which often prolong the grief process when this act of separation is not performed, and this is one of the problems with a memorial service. Death is commemorated by a rite of passage; the removal of the casket from the public gathering and the placing of it in the grave or crematory are important parts of the rite. Any attempt to deny the reality of separation is not a service to the bereaved but frequently a real disservice. The finality is underlined better by the actions of the disposal of the body than by anything said in the service.

Christian burial, then, has several important functions: to proclaim the power of God, to give thanks for a specific life, to support the bereaved, to commend the deceased to God, and to dispose of the body. All these must be considered as we plan space for the service of Christian burial.

Funeral Spaces

What kinds of spaces do we need for these functions? The needs, for the most part, are similar to those of the normal Sunday service, but a few important concerns need careful attention. Chief among these is the scale of a casket — about three feet by six feet — with the important differences that, unlike the normal human figure, it is horizontal and must be moved by others, usually several others. These changes in scale inform our discussion at every point.

When we plan actual spaces for a service of Christian burial, we need to begin with the place for the casket. Most churches have moved away from the practice of having the casket open during any part of the service, so it is no longer necessary to have it parallel to the altar-table and pews; it can remain in the aisle, perpendicular to both. Often, it is directly in front of the altar-table but at a lower level. Concern must be taken that communion rails, when present, do not block this location. There should be enough space between the altar-table and the first rows of pews that the casket and all that accompanies it will not be crowded.

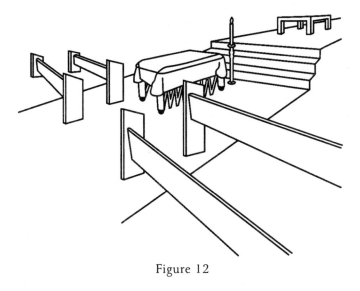

Figure 12

Where the baptismal font is near the front of the church, space for the casket is sometimes provided there. Many new burial rites articulate the connection between baptism and burial: "As in baptism *Name* put on Christ, so in Christ may *Name* be clothed with glory." One Roman Catholic church — St. Charles Borremeo in London — has been renovated so that the casket rests immediately over the sunken baptismal pool in the middle of the central aisle. Frequently the paschal candle, a symbol of the resurrection, will be placed at the end of the casket.

With the casket not open, it is best to have a funeral pall available to cover it. These are of cloth, about six by ten feet, and may be ordered from church-supply stores or made locally. Usually the form of the cross occupies the center and white or green have become the common colors, suggesting continued growth in Christ. The pall removes the need for floral displays on top of the casket and covers the differences between expensive and less-costly caskets; in this sense, all are shown equal before God.

More important, it makes a clear connection between the cross, the central symbol of Christian faith, and the body of the deceased, something cut flowers can hardly do. The placement of floral displays, usually along the communion rails or steps, should be planned. These should not conceal the altar-table, pulpit, or font, which have their own witness to make. Frequently it is desirable to have floor candlestands, with a single candle each, placed at the four comers of the casket. The paschal candle or a processional cross may stand at the end of the casket nearest the altar-table.

A major symbolic action of this service is the bringing in and taking out of the casket. The central aisle must be wide enough to permit the casket and people carrying it to pass. Even when it is wheeled in and out, there often will be a procession and recession of pallbearers, choir, and clergy for whom sufficient space is necessary. Unfortunately, many churches have been designed without thought to the difficulties of getting a casket in and out in a horizontal position. Steps are inconvenient, whether it is carried or wheeled, especially when there is a rail down the middle over which it must be lifted (or slid in undignified fashion). Sharp turns cannot be negotiated easily if stairs or corridors turn with less than a six-foot radius. Careful planning of such routes makes funerals much easier to conduct with dignity.

Certain furnishings are necessary for the service of Christian burial. Much of the service will focus on the pulpit; other parts, on the altar-table. Scripture forms a major portion of the rite. God's comforting Word carries more authority when read from the pulpit. There may also be provision for an informal naming or witness to the specific life being commemorated. This often takes place before the altar-table, and when the Eucharist is celebrated at funerals, the congregation may receive communion. This demands careful planning so communicants or those distributing communion can move past the casket. In some cases, it may be best for the central aisle to be wider at the very front to accommodate the casket and this movement.

The church will need certain items, and storage space must be provided for them. Once churches found it necessary to store a bier, or catafalque, but the funeral director usually supplies this today; interestingly, this portable device is called a 'church truck.' Appropriate floor candlestands, which may be those usually used about the altar-table, a processional cross, the paschal candle, and the funeral pall are the responsibility of the church. It is often convenient to have small, inconspicuous tables for flowers, although florists sometimes bring stands.

The gathering space (or foyer or vestibule) has special functions in this service, especially as a place to greet the family and friends not seen for some time. Some of the floral decorations may be placed here. It is often desirable to have a table here in order that friends of the deceased and family may sign a book. In some communities, especially when the calling hours have been held at a funeral home at some distance from the church, this area is used as a place where persons may view the body prior to the service.

Some funeral homes have special rooms for the family, thus segregating them from the rest of the worshipers. This ought not to be copied in designing church space, since the presence of the supportive congregation is a primary symbol; the family, though it may occupy special pews, should be in and with the community as closely as possible. A separate room for members of the family to gather and prepare themselves before and after the services is sometimes desirable.

In recent years a few churches (for instance, St. Elizabeth Seton in Carmel, Indiana) have designed space for wakes. This can easily be done in a weekday or eucharistic chapel. Space for the open casket to be viewed may be provided at one side. A *prie-dieu* should be available for people to kneel in prayer as they view the body.

Places for burial will be discussed in chapter 8, but we may make a few comments here on exterior space. The roofed medieval lichgate, where the pastor met the casket and preceded it into the church, is rarely copied in this country and less often actually used. But it does serve to remind us that the service of Christian burial is not limited to the building. Indeed, the rite itself involves passing over a very important threshold, signifying separation from the living community that has its focus in the building. One sets out on the last journey by coming home to the familiar place of worship before departing forever.

In our culture, interment usually occurs elsewhere, and this requires departure by car. Space for the parking of hearse, family car, and cars of the mourners should be carefully planned for ease of access, especially for the elderly and infirm. Sometimes this space is reserved with movable signs. Movement from church threshold to hearse must be thought out so that it can be done with both dignity and convenience.

SEVEN

A PLACE FOR
CHURCH MUSIC

Of all human languages, music is one of the most powerful and evocative. We use music in our celebration and in our lament. We use it to express our deepest joys and most profound sorrows. Throughout human history, music also has been one of the languages with which we express the richness of our relationship with God. Indeed, because music is such an intangible thing, here one minute and gone the next, it has been considered the most "spiritual" of all the arts, and somehow especially appropriate for the worship of God.

As Christians, we have found music an appropriate way to express our faith, and part of our common memory is the worship of God through music. We learn in Scripture how significant music was for the Jewish people in their worship. We find Miriam singing a song of joy to celebrate the deliverance of her people from slavery in Egypt (Exod. 15). We find King David commanding the Levites to appoint singers and instrumentalists to "raise the sounds of joy" (1 Chron. 15:16), and the admonition "Sing to the Lord!" appears throughout the Old Testament narrative (e.g., Exod. 15:21; Jer. 20:13). Most significant is the fact that one entire book, the book of Psalms, is a songbook, a hymnal for those who worship the God of Israel.

The earliest followers of Jesus seem to have adopted the Jewish tradition of giving an important place to liturgical music, although New Testament evidence is slim. The most familiar reference is probably the passage from Ephesians (5:18b-19), in which the writer teaches the church at Ephesus what to do when it gathers for worship: "Be filled with the Spirit, addressing one another in psalms and hymns and spiritual songs, singing and making melody to the Lord with all your heart." We can find some of these "hymns" scattered throughout the New Testament (Mark 14:36; Eph. 5:14; I Tim. 3:16; I Tim. 6:15). In one of the most beautiful passages (Luke 1:46b-55), Mary sings a hymn of praise: "My soul magnifies the Lord, and my spirit rejoices in God my Savior!"

Throughout the following centuries, music continued to be a vehicle for both Christian praise and Christian theology. Although music changed as the Church and the world around it changed, all Christian traditions, to a greater or lesser degree, have found in music a profound and vital religious vocabulary. Plainchant and polyphony, Lutheran chorales and English hymns, romantic masses and Black spirituals — all are a part of the rich tapestry that is the musical expression of the church's faith.

But music is not part of the worship life of the Christian community for its own sake — its beauty, its virtuosity, or its entertainment value. Rather, music gives voice to the praises and prayers of the Christian people. Its special power in worship is that it can reach so deeply into the human heart that it can enable us to say not only what we think but what we feel. Music builds and strengthens the bonds of the Christian community. Joining with one another in music unites us in more profound ways than does joining in speech or in gesture. We give ourselves over to the music and, in so doing, to one another.

Because music is such a powerful means of expression, it also carries with it the potential for creating division within the Christian community. Some of the most bitter battles have been fought over the issue of which music is most adequate for the worship of God. Any committee charged with the preparation of a new denominational hymnal faces a barrage of letters — "Don't take this-or-that hymn away from us!". The language we use about our church music is intensely personal, intensely emotional, and for most of us, the experience of church is closely wedded to the experience of church music.

In all candor, we must say that music also will provide the source for much controversy in any church building or renovation project. Musicians usually are the most organized and cohesive body in any congregation, and they frequently prevail in discussions of such crucial matters as location of the choir or position of the organ console. The visual and functional aspects of the building rarely have such staunch and enthusiastic advocates. Just as an hour-long service is very often shaped to provide a proper setting for a few minutes of choral music, so too is the building as a whole shaped to provide a setting for the makers of music. We can cite a number of church buildings that have been ruined visually by giving undue prominence to the choir and organ. Church building and renovating are truly political processes; it is up to the leadership of any congregation to ensure that all constituencies have equal access to decision-making in this process.

Congregational Song

Several of the ways music is used in Christian worship have serious implications for shaping the space in which Christian worship occurs. Sometimes music makes demands on the worship space that are different from, or even in conflict with the demands made by other elements of worship. It is important that the church building enable every person present to offer his or her ministry of music.

The heart of Christian church music is congregational song, the Christian community raising its voice in praise of God, gaining an added depth and richness from its participation in worship. For most Protestants, including Lutherans and Anglicans, song is most fully realized in the hymn, in sacred poetry set to music. Our denominational hymnals become valued companions and guides in our journey in faith.

Since congregational song is so important, the architecture of the church building should do everything possible to facilitate it, to allow the congregation to sing at its best. It is important that people who are not confident singers feel they are singing with others. If they do not hear others around them, it is likely that they will simply keep quiet.

The church building can do a great deal to promote the fullness of sound that encourages, rather than inhibits, congregational singing. For the most full-bodied sound, the congregation should be massed in a rather circumscribed area. Small groups segregated in balconies, alcoves, or transepts feel less courageous about singing out than do larger bodies that are together in one space. In this way, individual voices are supported by sound from all sides.

Psalmody is another kind of congregational song that has important implications for the arrangement of worship space. The singing or chanting of psalms, which are the common property of both Christians and Jews, has a central place in Christian worship. The lectionary provides one psalm per day for Sunday worship, as many as twelve for some occasions. Very often in Sunday worship, as well as in special services, the psalms may be sung or chanted antiphonally. A given piece of music is divided, and the sections are sung alternately by two or more groups. (In the case of psalms, this usually involves a division into verses or parts of verses.)

In a worship space ideally suited to antiphonal singing, the seating should be capable of being easily separated into two sections, preferably with the potential for those sections to face each other. The traditional "collegiate" arrangement of the school or monastic chapel is exactly in this pattern, because antiphonal singing of psalms made up the bulk of worship life in such places. Often it is impossible for the main worship space to be permanently arranged in this manner, but a weekday chapel (cf. chap. 8), where the singing or chanting of psalms is a regular event, might profitably be designed with two blocks of seating which confront each other across an aisle.

The congregation also takes a principal part in the singing of responses, usually relying on the cues of one person—the presider, cantor, song leader, clerk, or reader. The presider, for example, may sing "The Lord be with you," and the congregation will respond, "And also with you." Or the cantor or reader may sing a line, which is then repeated by the entire congregation. These responses ought to flow naturally between the leader and congregation, with no break in the dialogue between them. Because visual cues (arm or hand gestures, for example) are often used, it is important that the entire congregation be able to see the leader easily. Since this practice of singing responses is heavily dependent upon auditory cues, the leader also must be able to be heard by the entire congregation.

The singing of service music is another part of the musical ministry of the congregation. Service music is defined as those unvarying portions of Christian worship which traditionally have been given musical settings: *Kyrie* ("Lord, have mercy"), *Gloria Patri* ("Glory to the Father"), *Gloria in excelsis* ("Glory to God in the highest"), *Te Deum* ("You are God: we praise you"), the *Sanctus* ("Holy, holy, holy"), the *Agnus Dei* ("Lamb of God") and various doxologies (such as "Praise God from Whom All Blessings Flow") are most common. Sometimes the Apostles' Creed and the Lord's Prayer are sung by the congregation. Like other forms of liturgical response, the singing of service music relies on the ability of the congregation to see and hear the person who gives the cue lines. If the people are unable to do so, there will be an uncertainty about the congregational participation and an artificiality about the liturgical conversation.

Choral Music

In much of the history of Christian worship, we find the existence of bodies of singers who assist in the musical ministry of the church. These groups, most often called choirs, are made up of individuals who have a gift and want to offer that gift for the use of the Christian community. But different communities of Christians have different understandings about the role of a choir within their worship.

Given that the primary musical ministry in the church belongs to the congregation, the most important role for the choir is that of enabling the whole congregation to offer its own ministry of music to the best of its ability. In other words, with its special training and musical ability, the choir offers itself as an aide to the congregation's own ministry of music. This brings us directly to the architectural question: Where can the choir be located so that it best fulfills this role?

There are several possibilities for the location of a choir that would enable it to function as a support system for the singing community. The first is to place it at the rear of the congregation, either on the same level as the main section of congregational seating or in a balcony. The advantage of this location is that the sound the choir produces comes to individuals in the congregation from behind, and thus is able to provide a great deal of support. Placing the choir at the rear of the congregation has the added advantage of allowing the choir to do its work without calling unnecessary attention to itself. On the other hand, located in the rear, especially in a gallery or balcony, the choir may feel it is segregated from the community rather than an integral part of it and if the choir is needed to give the congregation visual cues to the liturgical action, it is unable to do so.

A second location forges a compromise, allowing the choir to support the singing of the congregation by massing together to form a solid body of sound, yet also allowing it to feel itself a part of the congregation. This is the placement of the choir in a section of ordinary congregational seating on the main floor of the church building. To identify this seating as choir space, it can be raised a step or two from floor level, but not so much as to isolate the choir. For the most emphatic support of the community's singing, this area should run from back to front of congregational seating, rather than from side to side.

There is yet another and perhaps more daring placement for the choir within the worshiping community, one that has a number of distinct advantages. The idea here is to disperse the members of the choir, "planting" them throughout the congregation and allowing the singing of each to influence a small section of the community. This works well in small, informal congregations, but also can succeed in larger ones, especially if there are many choristers and they are well trained and rehearsed. Although the choir in this case is not vested, it rehearses as usual so that all the music is familiar. To adopt this "location" allows choir members to sit with their families during worship (which may ultimately increase choir membership) and to offer their worship with the whole congregation.

Although the primary ministry of the choir is to enable the music ministry of the whole congregation, there are other valid, albeit secondary, roles for the choir in Christian worship. Often the choir is charged with offering music that demands a higher level of talent and training than the congregation possesses. In this capacity the choir sings on behalf of the congregation, so that a whole range of the very best of Christian music can be a part of the worship of God in this particular place and time. Here the choir serves as teacher, allowing the congregation to hear and learn new and more difficult pieces of music. But for the most part, acting as a musical surrogate for the congregation means that the choir sings independently, with the congregation exercising its participation vicariously. Traditionally, the most common form of choral singing is the choir anthem.

There is no reason for this role to disallow any of the three options for the choir's location. It is not necessary that the choir be seen to fulfill the function of singing on behalf of the congregation, only that it be heard. In the third option, in which the choir is dispersed throughout the congregation, members of the choir can simply move to a common place for the singing of the anthem, then return to their seats.

In a few churches there is one rather limited function of the choir which demands that it be seen as well as heard. In communities that have very elaborate ceremonial, the choir occasionally will be trained and used to give cues, guiding the congregation in its liturgical gestures. This may be the one case in which a highly visible choir might be tolerated but it certainly can function from the least prominent location.

Generally, architectural plans that locate the choir at the front, facing the congregation, are not a reasonable option for the average Christian community. This placement harkens back to the days when the choir was viewed primarily in terms of its entertainment value, or as a device for manipulating the feelings or mood of worshipers. When the choir sings in such a location, we cannot help feeling we are the "audience," with the choir on stage and those of us in the congregation passive onlookers. In addition, the choir that confronts the congregation is usually a visual distraction, diverting attention from the primary actions of worship that take place at the altar-table, the pulpit, and the font. Given these serious difficulties, it is not surprising that many recent church renovation projects have focused on the elimination of the concert-stage arrangement.

But there is an important exception to this trend. We spoke above about the architectural setting for antiphonal singing, and in one particular tradition the placement of othe choir contributes to what is, essentially, a service which is entirely antiphonal. In the African-American traditions of worship, the choir is almost invariably placed at the front in a concert-stage arrangement, not to indicate its status as 'performer,' but as one-half of an antiphonal congregation. The congregation and choir exchange both sung and spoken responses, and both visual and audotiry cues between the two are essential to the liturgical action.

Suffice it to say that the question of the location of the choir is one of the most vexing problems in building and renovating for Christian worship. But because most congregations never have taken the time to analyze exactly how a choir functions in their worship, or how it ought to function, they have not based this decision on a solid foundation. If we view the choir as simply a showpiece, we will be led to certain conclusions about its location. However, if we begin with the model of the choir as a servant for the music ministry of the whole congregation, we are sure to arrive at a very different solution.

Whatever location is chosen, several subsidiary requirements for choir space must be taken into account. Some are musical considerations, some are practical details, and some are aimed simply at allowing the choir to worship as much as possible as part of the Christian community. Although they may seem insignificant, attention to these minor details can make choir singing a joy rather than a chore.

The first question to ask of choir space is, "How will the choir get in and out?" In some churches there is a tradition of a choir procession, although this is by no means a necessity. If there must be a choir procession in order to get the choir into its place in an orderly fashion, is the route direct and uncomplicated? Is there enough distance between the rows of seating to allow easy passage? Thee architecture of the building can turn strictly utilitarian action of the entry and exit of the choir into a major production if careful thought is not given to the path the procession will take.

There is a certain advantage to providing movable, individual chairs in the choir space, rather than fixed seating. With flexible seating, there can be the same number of seats as choristers, with no empty chairs, so that the space looks full no matter how many choir members are absent. Ample book racks are necessary, not only for music but for Bibles, service books, hymnals, bulletins all the things necessary for the choir to worship with the congregation. These racks can be attached to the backs of chairs (to be used by the person in the chair behind), underneath the chairs several inches off the floor, or on the side(s) of each chair. If kneeling is the custom, kneelers should also be provided for the choir members, again so they are able to enter into the community's worship as fully as possible. The tendency of moveable chairs to look disorderly when not being occupied can be avoided by designing them to be 'ganged' solidly together.

Ability to see the choir director from each seat is, of course, crucial. This may involve providing either a podium for the director or risers (graded platforms) for the choir. Equally important is the ability of the choir to see and hear what is going on in the rest of worship. In that way, the choir parts will flow naturally into the liturgical action. Members of the choir should also be able to see and hear one another, which can help enormously in keeping the music in tune and in time.

Although it is not usually a part of the main worship space, adequate rehearsal space for the choir can help all the various ministries of music function more smoothly. This room should be spacious and well lighted, so that long periods spent reading music are not tiring. Seating should provide good back support and should be placed so that singers can see and hear both the director and one another. In most cases, a piano of good quality is the preferred rehearsal instrument. And the acoustics of the rehearsal room should be agreeable to music.

Ample storage space is a necessity for the choir room. Large closets for vestments, music stands, and instrument cases; filing cabinets (or some other library system) for sheet music should be provided. In addition, there should be built-in boxes for each choir member, into which the music for each week's rehearsal is placed. A bathroom (or at least a source of running water), full-length mirrors, and bulletin boards are also useful elements in a well-equipped choir room. If an office for the director of music is provided, it should be located near the choir rehearsal space.

One other important consideration is the path the choir takes from its rehearsal room to the place where it enters the worship space. Occasionally a congregation has built or renovated worship space, thinking it has taken the choir into consideration, only to find that the choir is forced to walk some distance outside to arrive at the main church building. In certain climates this presents little difficulty, but in most of North America the weather cannot be relied upon to cooperate.

If a choir procession is traditional, the choir should have some convenient place to gather where the normal sounds made during the process of formation are not distracting to worshipers already seated in the church. If there is no procession, the choir should be able to enter easily and directly through a door near the choir space and take its place without calling undue attention to itself.

These details may seem insignificant in the face of a major building project, but careful attention to each can make a significant difference in the ability of the choir to serve the congregation well, now and in the future.

The Pipe Organ

The decision about the location and configuration of the choir space is intimately bound up with decisions about the church organ. For the better part of a thousand years, the pipe organ has been looked upon as the church's instrument, and it continues today to be a most satisfying and agreeable instrument for the support of congregational song, for the accompaniment of the choir, and as a solo performer in its own right. The church organ represents a major financial outlay for most congregations, and its purchase demands careful consideration. The wrong instrument for a particular church building can overwhelm both the space and the worship of the congregation. Wrongly placed, even the finest instrument can sound muffled and out of balance; wrongly placed, it can alter the entire focus of the worship space, distracting attention from the principal liturgical action. An organ can be the best investment a congregation can make. Or it can be the worst.

There are several important arguments for the purchase of a genuine pipe organ rather than an electronic device. Some arguments are aesthetic in nature, concerned with such matters as the quality of sound or the appearance of the casework. Some are more philosophical, dealing with the use of an "imitation" in Christian worship, the electronic organ being a simulation of the genuine pipe organ. All these points of view are to be taken seriously, but for most building and finance committees, they do not always justify the extra expense of a pipe organ.

Therefore it is important to look at the economic arguments in favor of a pipe organ. First of all, such a purchase is a long-term investment. The oldest church organ in use is over eight hundred years old and still going strong. Even the best electronic devices will not last more than ten to fifteen years and many break down long before that. By the time the electronic organ has been replaced two or three times, a small pipe organ could have been paid for. In addition, a pipe organ holds its value, whereas only a tiny fraction of the original investment in an electronic device can generally be recovered.

The pipe organ can be installed one section at a time, with additional sections added as the needs of the community expand. With an electronic organ, one purchases what one can afford, and then when the demands of the community increase, the original instrument is discarded and the process begins all over again. Not only is this economically unsound but it also seems to make the community a willing participant in the disposable culture of the late twentieth century.

Each pipe organ is unique, designed for the particular space it will occupy and for the particular needs it will serve. Since it is tailored to the place and people who will use it, the congregation will derive the maximum benefit from it—the best sound for its dollar, so to speak. The electronic organ, on the other hand, is generally mass produced on the lowest-common-denominator principle, which means it never will be able to meet exactly the demands of any specific congregation. It will, in every case, either exceed or fall short of what is needed. Both these options are to be avoided, and both waste the congregation's money.

Many congregations make the mistake of comparing the cost of a new pipe organ to that of a new electronic device. Most fail to consider that a good second-hand organ will be more affordable than a newly built one and will have many, if not all of its advantages. A second-hand instrument will give years of service, and when more resources are available, the old instrument can be moved to a weekday chapel or the choir room, can serve as the heart of the new organ, or can be sold outright.

The final argument for a good pipe organ is that it will draw talented musicians to serve the community, whereas an electronic device may keep them away. Many fine organists simply will not accept a position in which they are expected to play an electronic organ week after week. Much important sacred literature has been written for the pipe organ, and many of the great choral masterworks rely on pipe-organ accompaniment. Although some of this music may be adapted to the limitations of the electronic organ, no church music has been written expressly for it.

There is, despite all these considerations, no rule that a community needs any sort of organ at all. Many congregations worship regularly, happily, and successfully without them; some actually forbid them. But for most, a church organ is viewed as the most desirable option; for many, as a virtual necessity. But what of the congregation that finds it absolutely impossible to purchase even the smallest pipe organ? What is its next best alternative?

Here many of the same economic arguments advanced for the purchase of a pipe organ also apply. What sort of instrument will hold its value and still be of use when the community does purchase a pipe organ? What sort of instrument will be emphatic enough to support congregational singing and perform the other functions connected with the role of music in the church?

For most congregations faced with this decision, a good piano is the most reasonable answer. A real piano is preferable to a simulated organ, for the same economic, musical, and aesthetic reasons that a real organ is preferable to an electronic one. Although a piano does not approach the range and versatility of the organ, it perhaps comes closest and should be considered as an alternative in instances where the purchase of a pipe organ is impossible or undesirable. Guitars or other such instruments, while possessing authenticity, are designed for solo voice accompaniment. They do not serve well in the essential functions of supporting congregational song and accompanying the choir.

In many recent church building projects, especially among the so-called 'mega-churches,' a pipe organ (and its literature) are not considered as a suitable or desirable accompaniment to the forms of worship being offered. The model for some is Robert Schuller's Crystal Cathedral, which has a number of fine organs installed. Yet, for most of these churches electronic instruments of various kinds — guitars, pianos, percussion sets — as well as recorded music, is the preferred option in an effort to make worship relevant to the musical tastes of the young, largely unchurched attenders. What the future of these experiments will be is difficult to forecast, but with the proliferation of these experiments, the death of the pipe organ as a church instrument has been predicted by some observers.

If the congregation does decide to purchase a pipe organ, its selection and positioning require an enormous amount of time and care and the consultation of many persons involved with the building process: architect, organ builder, organist, choir director. Many questions related to the location of the pipe organ will be matters of acoustical and structural engineering; many will be matters of overall design integrity; but some are simply matters of liturgical convenience.

In most cases, decisions regarding the positioning of the organ will be made together with decisions about the location of the choir. Lines of communication between choir and organ are vitally important, especially if the organist also serves as choir director and conducts from the organ console. Adequate sight lines between organist and presider, cantor, readers, and other participants in worship are necessary if the music is to flow naturally within the service. Often, elaborate systems of mirrors can be erected, but for the convenience of the organist, the fewer the better.

It is tempting for a congregation, having spent a large sum of money on a pipe organ, to place it in the front of the church where it can be seen, but this is a temptation to be avoided for several reasons. As was the case with the choir, the sound of the organ can most fully support congregational singing from behind. In addition, the organ in the front of the church can be as distracting from the principal liturgical action as is the choir placed in front. The church is not a concert hall, and the placement of the organ should never suggest that it is an object of worship. Some congregations make the opposite mistake and, having bought a fine pipe organ, proceed to bury it in organ chambers or alcoves where much of its sound is obscured. The sound of a pipe organ, like sound of any kind, travels best in straight lines, and if the organ is placed so that its sound must turn corners to reach the congregation or choir, much of its power and clarity will be lost.

If an electronic organ is chosen, the sound will be dependent on the positioning of external speakers. Again, the support of congregational singing will be the principal consideration in this task, and the elimination of 'dead zones' will be extremely important. In all of this, the advice of a professional acoustical engineer is supremely important in order that the expense of the instrument is not wasted by poor sound distribution.

Other Instruments

Other kinds of instruments often are used in Christian worship. Since this may involve anything from a single flute to a full orchestra (and every combination in between), it is important to think through the role of instrumental music in worship in order to provide sufficient space to accommodate it. Moreover, the shape of the space can be as important as the amount. A harpsichord may require the same square footage as a string trio, but the configuration of each space will be very different. For some kinds of music, such as gospel songs, space for a piano will be required.

Generally, it is impossible to provide for all conceivable options, but if instruments are to be a regular part of the community's worship, now or in the future, ample space should be provided for the comfort of the musicians. If other instruments are to support congregational singing or accompany choir or organ, again the matter of sight lines must be addressed. Usually, the space for other instrumentalists is made a part of the choir space and thus participates in the success or failure of the placement of the choir.

If electronic instruments are or may be used regularly, it is necessary to provide sufficient electrical outlets for the equipment, and perhaps space outside the worship space for sound-mixing and recording purposes. Often the person working with this equipment will need a way of seeing into the main worship space in order to coordinate the music with singers and choir. To avoid the need for long extension cords or multiple plugs in a single outlet, providing many points of access to the power supply is always better than providing just a few.

There are certain occasions other than the service of worship when the space designed for Christian worship is used for music. Sacred concerts, special musical services (the Advent "Service of Lessons and Carols," for example) and performances of religious opera or other drama are an important part of the life of certain Christian communities. In these cases, the dynamics of theater rather than those of worship are operative. Since congregational seating is transformed into audience seating on these occasions, the principal consideration is the ability to see and hear the action from all seats. Some congregations have sets of movable platforms which can be arranged in various configurations at the front of the church building. Some prefer to make even more space available by designing the communion rails, clergy seating, altar-table and other furnishings so that they can be easily removed and stored, leaving the entire chancel area open for the players. If religious drama or opera is a regular ac-

tivity of the congregation, wider aisles or extra space in front of
the first row of pews might be considered. A location from which
stage lighting is operated, and the fixtures and wiring to accommodate it, should be decided upon but made easily removable.
In addition, a place for the permanent storage of stage props,
music stands, costumes, and sets should be added to the plan.

Acoustics

Few factors are as invisible as acoustics and yet have such
massive influence on the character and quality of worship celebrated in a building. Acoustics can enable and enhance
congregational singing or almost destroy it. Bad acoustics can
make even the best preaching inaudible or ruin the majesty of
a pipe organ in which the congregation may have invested
hundreds of thousands of dollars. To the hearing-impaired and
people for whom English is not a first language, attention paid
to the acoustics of a worship space can make all the difference
in their ability to participate meaningfully in corporate worship.

We do not propose to give a full explication of acoustics
here but simply point to some essential concerns and indicate
where and how to get help. If we can make the single point that
congregations need to be concerned enough over this item to
find the best professional help available, we shall be content.
Our chief concern is to suggest specific problems for which professional help frequently is necessary.

A useful approach is to think of a church interior as a musical instrument, which can sound quite different under different
circumstances: the size of the congregation present; the season
of the year, with sound drifting through open windows in the
summer and warmly dressed people in winter; the amount of
cushions, carpeting, and draperies present. Like a musical instrument, a church interior can be tuned. Ten minutes spent
removing pew cushions will make a distinct change in the way
sound behaves. The building is a sensitive instrument and
thoughtless handling can easily wreck its ability to provide a satisfactory acoustical environment.

As we have seen repeatedly, church design is a process of compromise, and this is certainly true with regard to acoustics. The essential conflict here is between an acoustical environment ideal for preaching, reading, and speaking and one that is ideal for vocal and instrumental music. The two types of sound require quite different environments. For the spoken word, the ideal space is one considered 'dry,' or 'dead,' with little reverberation and no echo. The time it takes for sound to disappear determines its 'dryness.' On the whole, soft surfaces—cushions, hanging fabrics, carpeting, human bodies—soak up sound quickly and cut down on reverberation. In contrast, hard surfaces—wood, plaster, brick, tile or stone—allow sound to bounce around a bit before it vanishes. As an experiment, clap your hands or shout in an empty building and note how many seconds it takes for the sound to disappear totally. In a very lively building, it may take several seconds.

A building which is very 'lively' can be difficult for preachers and speakers who want to be heard clearly. In worship space with a long reverberation time, the sound of the spoken words lingers in the air and mingles with the sound of the words that follow, causing a blurring effect. The ideal acoustical environment for the musician, by contrast, is a space in which sound persists for two or three seconds (or more) in order to mix together, and so a lively space with ample reverberation is desired. So, compromises are necessary in designing the acoustical environment for worship.

These compromises may not need to involve an elaborate acoustical design process. Some simple design decisions, which would at first seem more related to questions of decoration than of sound, can make an enormous difference to the tuning of a room for the worship of the church. For example, the amount of soft surface can be restricted, especially by avoiding carpeting and draperies.

The choice of floor covering can be a highly complex process. Many people argue that carpeting adds necessary warmth to a church interior, and absorbs the sound of people moving to and from their seats. Carpeting which covers the entire floor, may not be the most cost-effective choice for churches on a bud-

get, requiring as it does regular cleaning and periodic replacement. Wood, slate, brick, or tile floors are more durable, and
although these usually involve greater initial expense they may
prove less expensive in the long term. And, of course, carpeting
absorbs enormous amounts of sound.

There are some good compromises now available. New 'acoustical' carpeting materials are designed to provide the look and
feel of carpeting without its serious sound-absorbency problems.
The floor of a church building need not be covered with a single
material. Carpeting in the aisles and chancel area can cover the
sound of foot traffic and aid speaking from the front of the church;
this can be combined with a much harder surface under the pews
and in the choir area which can enhance the reverberation needed
for good congregational singing and music-making.

Some architectural features can be unfavorable for all kinds
of sound, both musical and the spoken word. Curved walls or
ceilings can cause echoes, or focus sound in certain spaces and
cause dead spots in others. Domes and vaulted ceilings may be
beautiful to the eye but can be catastrophes for the ear. When
such shapes are being planned, it is essential that the acoustic
consequences be well understood, or expensive remedies may
become necessary afterward. It is now possible to construct buildings that are tunable, with acoustical clouds overhead and
movable louvers that can change a wall from a soft surface to a
hard one in a matter of minutes.

It is tempting to try to remedy problems in acoustics by
using sound amplification for the preacher. With good acoustical planning, this can be avoided in small buildings. Persons who
lead worship need to speak from various locations pulpit, chair,
font, altar-table, before the altar-table—and a microphone detracts from the design of any of these places. A clip-on microphone
has aesthetic advantages, but a long cord is a nuisance; a cordless
clip-on escapes these disadvantages, but even this should not be
necessary in buildings that seat three hundred or fewer people.
When it is necessary to have sound amplification, the loudspeaker
should be located so that sound comes from near the spot where
the person is speaking (such as over the pulpit), not from the
side walls or under the pews. Nor should the person speaking be

between the loudspeaker and the congregation, as some systems may pick up the amplified voice in addition to the natural voice. Again, the advice of an acoustical engineer is a wise investment.

Care with regard to the placement of the pipe organ is essential. Many congregations make their largest investment in such an instrument, then proceed to bury it or place it in such a location that the sound must make a sharp turn to reach the congregation. Organ chambers should speak directly to the congregation, not around corners. However, there are good reasons for not making the organ pipes the central visual object in the building an object of worship in their own right. Music coming from behind or beside the congregation can help encourage its singing. An electronic organ has fewer problems in terms of placement, but all of the factors we have noted about the choice and placement of sound-amplification systems apply here as well.

If these considerations sound complex, they are. We strongly advise any group considering building or renovating a church to employ a qualified acoustical consultant. We insist that these not be people who make a living from selling sound-amplification systems or sound-deadening materials, since those people usually can be relied upon to discover that a congregation needs precisely what they have to sell, whether that need is real or not. Acoustical consultants can be found in the engineering departments of most universities, or if not, someone there probably will know where a competent acoustical engineer can be found. Such people are well worth their hire since they may prevent expensive mistakes if contacted in time. They may not work miracles with mistakes already made, but sometimes can point to inexpensive ways to correct them. Before the architect goes into working drawings, however, the acoustical engineer should be contacted to consult with the users of the building and to insure that the sound in the church will function as intended.

EIGHT

SUBSIDIARY SPACES

Although the Sunday assembly for worship is the principal gathering of the local community of faith, increasingly we find Christians coming together at other times and for other purposes. In many churches, small groups meet for daily worship, for weeknight prayer meetings, or for special services of healing or reconciliation. Individuals may seek a place for meditation and reflection. Families may wish somewhere in or near the church to bury and to remember their dead and group retreats or midweek Communion services are regular offerings in the programs of many churches. Just as a house must be designed to accommodate a family's varied activities, so too must the house for the church be shaped around the needs of the Christian family for which it is built.

Different possibilities exist for accommodating these activities within the church structure, but in general, the solution will follow one of two patterns. In the first, space for all church activities is incorporated into the main worship area of the church. This solution has two distinct advantages. First, shaping a single space to meet a variety of needs is less costly than building a separate space for each individual demand. The second advantage to confining all the community's activities to one space is that we are always reminded, be it Wednesday evening at prayer or Friday morning in private meditation, that our primary relationship is to the Christian community as a whole, gathered for worship on Sunday, the day of the Resurrection.

The second way to accommodate the varied ways the community comes together during the week is to provide a number of smaller spaces away from the main worship area, each tailored expressly for a specific function. This approach also has advantages.

In colder climates where heating costs are a factor, the ability to heat smaller spaces on a when-used basis is more economical than heating the whole worship-space for each occasion on which people gather. In some churches security is a concern, and the main church must be kept locked to protect it from theft or vandalism. In this case, a weekday chapel can be safely left open while the rest of the building is secured. These smaller spaces for subsidiary activities also have the benefit of a more profound sense of intimacy when a small group is gathered; a coherent community is thus more easily achieved.

In all but the most extensive building or renovation projects, however, the solution to shaping the church building to meet this wide variety of needs will very likely be a creative combination of these two approaches. For some gatherings (mid-week celebrations of the Lord's Supper and daily services, for example) the main worship area may be quite suitable, especially in small churches. For other purposes, such as private devotions and reconciliation or services of Christian burial, separate space such as a smaller weekday chapel may be required. But in any case, the needs of the community and the purposes for which it gathers that should always be the main consideration in making decisions about the allocation of space within the church building.

Daily Prayer

Increasingly, Christian communities see the value of gathering to pray together not only on Sunday mornings but during the week as well. Daily prayer for the Christian is a response to what Paul saw to be the heart and center of Jesus' teaching: "Pray continually" (1 Thess. 5:17). In marking the course of the day with prayer, one becomes aware that all time belongs to God and is to be used in the service of God. Early Christians found, as did devout Jews, that certain times during the day naturally lent themselves to dialogue with God. Traditionally, Christians have prayed, together or individually, at rising, midday, in the evening, and before retiring for the night.

This course of prayer often occurs in families or in other close-knit communities such as monasteries. Occasionally hospitals and retreat centers will mark their days with prayer and praise of God. But more and more Christians are coming together out of the business of their daily lives to meet for prayer at their local church and in a number of mainline denominations services for this purpose have been published. These services highlight the sense that the course of daily prayers (often referred to as the "daily office," "divine office," or "liturgy of the hours") is flexible and responsive to the whole range of needs, concerns, and gifts each day presents. Since these services can be led by lay people, they often do not require time out of a pastor's already busy schedule. The official services for daily prayer take into account not only regular daily worship but the many other circumstances in which Christian communities may wish to come together for prayer during the week.

The heart of the traditional daily service is prayer, the reciting of psalms, and, to a lesser extent, readings from Scripture. Traditionally, daily prayer services are less variable than other services, giving people an opportunity to become quickly familiar with them and to find in them a recurring rhythm of prayer and praise. Rather than being closely tied to the church year, the daily office allows the time of day to determine its character and content. Morning devotions are focused on praise of God and thanksgiving for God's creation. At evening prayer, we reflect on the day past, on God's gifts and the way we have used them, and on petitions for the needs of others. Noonday prayer, particularly in large city churches, provides a time of quiet during a busy day to recall our dependence upon God and our need to put all our work at God's disposal.

Shaping a separate space for the daily office alone is not difficult; the only absolute necessity is seating. This seating may be placed either facing forward, in a circle or semicircle, or, as is common when the psalms are read antiphonally, in parallel rows facing each other across an aisle (the "collegiate" arrangement mentioned earlier). Large groups may require a lectern, from which readings and prayer can be better heard. If the piety of the community demands it, kneelers may also be appropriate. A stand for a single large candle for evening services, and space for musicians and their instruments is also desirable.

Very often the space for the daily office will be used not only for weekday prayer services but for any occasion when a smaller group may wish to gather in the church. Such a space, generally referred to as a 'weekday chapel,' may serve for everything from a mid-week Lord's Supper to choir practice. For this reason it probably needs to be the most flexible space in the entire church building. One way to achieve this flexibility is with movable seating, which allows for a traditional forward-facing arrangement for Holy Communion, a collegiate plan for antiphonal psalmody, wider aisles for small weddings or funerals, and groupings of chairs for private devotion or Bible study classes, all within the same space.

Other furnishings also will be needed if the space is to suit a variety of uses. A weekday chapel that will be used for a mid-week Lord's Supper (or smaller Sunday celebration) will need an altar-table in scale with its surroundings and should possess the other characteristics outlined in chapter 3. A place from which the lessons may be read and a homily preached may be required (see chap. 2). Access to the sacristy and a source of running water will add to the utility of the space.

Devotions

In all ages, Christians have found comfort and spiritual nourishment by simply being in a place associated with the gathering of the Christian community and the presence of God. Many individuals feel they can better focus their spiritual attention while praying in the church building, itself alive with memories of Christian worship and images of the faith. It has always been the case, however, that pursuit of a deeper personal relationship with God and a clearer understanding of God's will is undertaken for the sake of the community and its ministry to all the world, not for some private benefit. The believer who prays in solitude is still a part of the community of faith, and a feeling for place often reflects this belonging.

But because spaces for devotions are designed to serve a more personal and subjective experience, they usually are better located away from the main worship space, which is designed to enhance corporate experiences. Often the weekday chapel can serve this purpose, but in many churches a completely separate and somewhat smaller space is provided. For most Protestant churches, all that may be necessary is a quiet place away from church traffic, perhaps with one good piece of visual art—sculpture, tapestry, or painting—on which devotional attention can be focused.

In the Roman Catholic, Eastern Orthodox, and certain segments of the Anglican tradition, other kinds of objects and activities have come to have devotional significance. Providing for these makes special demands on the ingenuity of a community. Records from the early days of Christianity tell us of pilgrims to Jerusalem who sought out and followed Jesus' last journey from the house of Pontius Pilate to Calvary. The desire to reenact their experience once they returned home led to the development of visual representations of that journey. Eventually the number of these images, or 'stations of the Cross,' was distilled to fourteen, which depicted scenes from Gospel accounts and from popular tradition. To these became attached large numbers of unofficial prayers and hymns, used both as aids to private meditation and as public devotions.

With the resurgence of a theology centered more on the resurrection than on the passion of Jesus, many churches have reevaluated the need for stations. In those communities that have decided to retain them, stations have become far less prominent. Most have chosen to place them outside the main worship area, believing their presence diverts attention away from the communal celebration of the liturgy. Some churches that have left the stations within the main worship space have reduced them to simple crosses set into the wall or floor, serving as reminders that the Christian life as a whole is a journey. Frequently a fifteenth station, the Resurrection, is now added.

One very successful alternative has been to place the stations of the cross outside the church building in a courtyard or along a landscaped walkway. However, since it is often older parishioners for whom this form of devotion is most meaningful, this solution works best in more moderate climates. Placing the stations in a weekday chapel is a possible compromise but retains the same disadvantages as placement in the main worship space, especially if the chapel is used often for daily Holy Communion or the daily office. Whatever their location, the images should be simple and direct, more in the nature of icons than illustrations (see chap. 9).

In some of the earliest accounts of the celebration of the Lord's Supper, we are told that a portion of the bread and wine from the Sunday eucharist was saved ("reserved") to be taken to the sick and to others who were not able to join with the whole community. As the reverence accorded to this eucharistic bread increased, the place where it was kept (tabernacle, aumbry, pyx, or sacrament house) began to take on greater visual prominence as prayerful attention was directed toward the elements within it. During the course of centuries, the tabernacle gradually became an important visual and devotional focus of the church building and the original purpose of reserving the elements within it for the sick was obscured.

Recent theological work has helped the church recover the understanding of the reserved elements as the means by which absent members can share in the celebration of the Lord's Supper with the whole community. Nevertheless, because the eucharistic bread is so closely associated with the presence of Jesus Christ, many Roman Catholics and Anglicans find meditation upon it a source of comfort and assurance.

As with other devotional elements, the reserved Sacrament as a devotional element is probably best located outside the main worship space, or any space (such as a weekday chapel) where the Lord's Supper is celebrated with regularity, since its devotional use is always derivative from and secondary to the eucharistic gathering of the community as a whole. The reserved Sacrament may occupy the same space as the stations of the cross, or another area set apart especially for private meditations.

Some churches have the tradition of vigil lights. Like other purely devotional objects, these are best kept away from the main worship space. Many communities are finding creative substitutes (such as tapers set into sand-filled clay pots) for the usual metal racks with votive candles. Electric imitations as substitutes for candles, devotional or other, have no place in a church.

As one can see, the difficulty in moving any or all of these out of the main worship space or weekday chapel is that one tends to multiply devotional items in a smaller space, thus unnecessarily distracting the prayerful attention of the individual. The alternative—to place the stations, reserved Sacrament, vigil lights, and meditation area in separate locations in the church—begins to become costly. Increasingly, communities are asking which of the many devotional items are most meaningful to them and are choosing to forego the others for the sake of simplicity.

Burials

The Christian Church is rightly called a 'communion of saints.' Christians understand by this that the church is comprised not only of the disciples of Jesus living on earth at any given time, but also those who have lived and died in ages past. We all, both living and dead, are members of the household of faith and members of Jesus Christ. For this reason, throughout the centuries Christians have considered the places they bury their dead to be worthy of special reverence. In times past, burial places were located in or near churches themselves, so that week after week the community continued to gather as one, even though separated by death.

With the advent of a more mobile society, a modern funeral industry, and the prices of urban real estate, burial sites in this country have been moved away from church buildings. In many cases this has led to an unfortunate diminishing of a sense of unity with our brothers and sisters in the faith who have gone before us. It is difficult for urban and suburban cemeteries and funeral homes, often separated from the church building by great distances, to retain their meaning as places of Christian worship when no other form of worship except the burial service is ever conducted there.

There are signs that this trend is being reevaluated, and some churches are again making provision for burial of their dead in or around the church building. Often this has required a certain amount of teaching and pastoral care aimed at overcoming modern squeamishness about grave sites, but churches in which the effort has been made have found the process rewarding. In some churches, remembrance of the dead is being provided for in other ways, but in all cases it is an effort to return to the sense of the Christian Church as a communion of both living and dead in Christ.

Burial sites in and around church buildings are of two kinds: those that accommodate bodies (the 'graveyard' or 'cemetery') and those that accommodate remains after cremation (generally called *columbaria*). To establish a graveyard on the grounds of a church requires long-range landscape planning, permission from local authorities, and some considerable space. Since it will serve both as the final resting place for members of the Christian community and as a place for family meditation and quiet reflection, it should be screened from auto and foot traffic as much as possible. Headstones and monuments, if present, should express the Christian message of hope in the Resurrection.

The other possibility for burial on the church site, and one with more appeal for churches with limited space or financial resources, is the provision of a place for interment of cremated remains, either within the church building or outside on the grounds. If such a place is desired within the building, a room can be set apart, or the walls and floor of the weekday chapel, church entrance, or crypt may be used. Occasionally, especially when one is designing an entirely new church building, the walls or floor of the main worship space can be constructed to accommodate a columbarium. In any case, removable floor or wall tiles that cover recesses of the necessary proportions, with space available for a permanent plate bearing the name and dates of the deceased, and perhaps a line from Scripture, are the only things necessary.

If the columbarium site is to be located in or around the exterior of the church, walkways (especially those leading to the main entrance) and the exterior walls can be used, but other locations unique to a given church situation can easily be adapted. Again, care must be taken that mourners and visitors are not disturbed by foot and auto traffic.

In providing space in or around one's church building for Christian burial, an unparalleled opportunity for expanding and deepening our understanding of the nature of the Christian church is presented. As Christians, we are a community of memory, and to come and go, to pray and sing, to be baptized and married in the presence of the whole community of faith, on earth and in heaven, gives our common life a richness many of us have sorely missed. Even if a given congregation should decide, for whatever reason, against the provision of a burial site in or around the church building, the discussion of the possibilities of such a plan, in and of itself, should be an opportunity for renewal and growth in a community.

Reconciliation

The Christian community, at its heart and center, is a community of reconciliation. It offers God's Word of reconciling love to all the world in the name of Jesus Christ and seeks in its own inner relationships to be a sign to all of that reconciliation. When as individual Christians we fall into sin, we turn to our brothers and sisters in Christ, who reassure us of the unfailing love of God. To repent, to confess, and to hear again God's promise of forgiveness, these form the core of reconciliation within the Christian community.

Over the centuries, the space within which this process occurs has undergone dramatic changes as our understanding of the process of reconciliation itself has changed. Among early Christians, serious sin, and thus reconciliation, were seen as grave concerns of the entire community. Penance, reconciliation, and reinstatement of the individual into full fellowship with the Christian community were matters conducted in public, with the community of faith playing an active role.

Gradually, sin began to be viewed as a private matter between the individual and God, and the clergy took on the role of mediator between the two parties. In Roman Catholicism, confession before a priest became common, especially as a way of preparing oneself to receive communion, and small booths, or confessionals, became a feature of most Roman Catholic church buildings. These confessionals assured the anonymity of the penitent and are still found in many Roman Catholic churches.

In recent years, however, we have begun to recover the importance of the human face of penitence and reconciliation, the sense that sin and forgiveness are never anonymous and that God works to reconcile us through human touch, human words, human gestures. This is the whole message of the Incarnation. In response to this reformed understanding of penance, communities have begun to see that space for reconciliation needs to be a human space, warm and hospitable, on a scale that invites human interaction. In those Protestant churches where sacramental penance is the practice, the pastor's study often serves as the place where it occurs. Many times, however, the necessary office routine, the interruptions, and the public location of the study make it a less than desirable place for reconciliation.

In many Roman Catholic church buildings, a separate "reconciliation room" is now provided, generally away from main traffic patterns. Comfortable seating and indirect lighting are the usual necessities, and for those individuals who continue to desire anonymity while making their confession, a portable screen may be set up and removed as needed. Other furnishings may include a *prie-dieu* or cushion on which to kneel for prayer or blessing and a devotional object such as a cross or statue. But in all furnishings, the ultimate goal is a sense of graciousness.

Often this sort of room can serve not only reconciliation but a multiplicity of pastoral-care needs. The effectiveness of marriage preparation, prayer with a bereaved family, healing, counseling all may be enhanced by an intimate setting such as the reconciliation room affords. In any case, whether these things take place in the pastor's study or a separate room, it is wise to think through the routes by which people come and go, so that those seeking pastoral attention will not feel they are being observed by others.

Sacristy and Storage

Within a church building there are numerous other areas which are not used directly for Christian worship or devotion, but act in service and support of the principal worship spaces. These areas make the various tasks accessory to worship easier, thus allowing people and clergy to concentrate on essentials. These architectural elements may be some of the less glamorous aspects of church design, but a congregation that pays sufficient attention to them will reap for itself ongoing benefits to its worship life.

One of the most important of these subsidiary spaces is the sacristy. The sacristy (in some places called the 'vestry') is the place in which the clergy and other worship leaders prepare for services, where those who are responsible for the setting of worship care for and make ready the various materials needed, and where flowers are prepared, and vestments, altar plate, banners, and other church furnishings are stored.

Anyone who has worked in a kitchen and pantry knows the advantage of ample and well-designed storage space. Of course, it is cooking, not storage, that the kitchen is all about, but with adequate storage space the cook can do the job more easily, enjoyably, and with a minimum of wasted effort. The same is true of the sacristy. Flat storage for altar linens, vestments, and banners, and hanging space for larger items such as funeral palls and altar frontals reduces the time spent ironing by a significant amount. Ample cupboard space is important for the storage of vessels used at or around the altar-table, communion ware, containers for flowers, and pitchers for baptism.

In addition, each community must think through its own unique needs for storage space. If there is an Advent wreath, where will it be put during the 47 weeks of the year when it is not in use? Where will the Christmas creche, candlestands, processional crosses, and candles be stored? Where will the pastor's coat and hat be hung? For each congregation, this list will be different. As each community begins to think about the design of safe, accessible, and ample storage facilities, it will be required to think about all the special items for the celebration of the church year or occasional services that are in use or may be used in the future. Security in the area may also be a consideration depending on local needs.

Larger items used only on an occasional basis also may need to be accommodated in the sacristy; the prie-dieu and runner for weddings and the bier for funerals are examples. In all cases, the sacristy and other subsidiary spaces should be built not only with the needs of the present in mind but also with an eye to the future.

As in the kitchen, the second important element in the sacristy is work space. For many tasks adequate counter space within easy reach of running water is a definite advantage. The arranging of flowers for use in worship and perhaps for taking to the sick after the service, the care of vestments, and the washing and polishing of communion ware are greatly facilitated by such an arrangement. Indeed, the provision of as much counter space as possible in the sacristy will certainly be profitable in making the care of items used in and around the main worship space a pleasure rather than a chore.

Other kinds of storage space besides that provided in a sacristy should also be considered in any church building or renovation project. In this era of crowded pew racks, space for the storage of books or papers used only occasionally in services would be of benefit to most congregations. We have already noted the importance of of storage space (for such things as hymnals, sheet music, music stands, and instruments) in and around the choir room (see chapter 7). Movable seating is a feature of many church buildings, and storage for it is essential. Flexible seating rapidly becomes permanent if there is nowhere to put it that is both easily accessible and away from main traffic areas when it is not needed.

The use of sophisticated electronic equipment in churches is becoming more common. If it is not permanently installed, some special storage considerations come into play. Beyond theft and damage concerns, some equipment needs to be stored in an environment where temperature and humidity are controlled. The provision of space for storing projection screens, scrims, speakers, and other accesories to electronic technology can consume large amount of space. Decisions on the purchase of any or all of these things must be made with an eye not only to the cost-benefit ratio of the equipment itself, but to storage and security as well.

Another storage area to be considered is the "broom closet," where the necessary supplies related to keeping the building clean are kept. Ample space for cleaning equipment and, if possible, a source of running water can make the job of keeping the building clean easier. Included in this space might be an area where cleaning supplies and lavatory items can be stockpiled so the church can take advantage of bulk purchase sales and other opportunities for savings.

Storage space should be provided for a small medical station, either in the sacristy or in a separate room near the main worship area. Equipped with first-aid supplies and instructions for emergency medical care, such a station can save valuable time during a health crisis. If this space can be located near a source of running water and a telephone with emergency numbers clearly posted, so much the better.

The provision of work and storage space may seem a secondary consideration when the building or renovation of a church is being undertaken, but it can make a major difference in preparing for worship, and thus a significant difference in the quality of the worship itself. To return to the analogy of the kitchen: When food is prepared and served in a gracious and unhurried way, and the environment in which food it eaten is given care and attention, then the whole experience of dining is enhanced. In the same way, even the smallest details of worship are of great significance to the experience of uniting in prayer with the Christian community. Insofar as work and storage space provides for attention to those details, it serves a principal role in enabling the worship of the church to be an experience that is rich and meaningful.

NINE

SPECIAL CONCERNS

In this chapter we shall treat several concerns of special importance that have no relation to individual services, or even to distinct parts of the church building. Yet many of these concerns affect all decisions about the various services of worship and about most portions of the building. Most are not obtrusive, yet failure to take them into consideration can result in buildings with serious deficiencies. All must be faced by committees and architects involved in church building or renovating, and all will necessitate important decisions.

These topics are widely varied — lighting, energy conservation, historic preservation, security, handicapped access, liturgical art, and memorial gifts.

Lighting

Planning the lighting in a church is far more than a purely functional matter — it is both an art and a science. Indeed, the quality of the entire environment for worship will be heavily shaped by the provision made for lighting. Harsh light can spoil the best interior; inadequate lighting can make hymn singing virtually impossible; and light in the wrong places may defeat or confuse the functions of the various spaces and centers.

We might distinguish between the issues of quantity and quality. Quantity of lighting is the matter of providing sufficient illumination in congregational space so that everyone, even those with impaired eyesight, can read the bulletin, hymnal, Bible, or service book without difficulty. Since many of these materials are in small print, fairly bright light is needed at pew level, and the same requirement applies to choir space. A high degree of illumination is also necessary for reading at the pulpit, altar-table, and baptismal font or pool, and also so that the actions of the persons leading worship are clearly visible to all. Similar intensity is not necessary in other places such as gathering space, where subdued lighting may seem more inviting, or in movement space, unless there are stairways.

On the other hand, glare from too much light can be a serious problem, especially if the congregation faces directly into it. Intense sunlight in the eyes of the congregation from a south-facing window can be downright painful, especially when the leaders of worship are silhouetted against the light. Besides allowing too much light to enter, picture windows tend to focus the attention of the congregation elsewhere rather than on the actions of the gathered community. We do not gather to witness spectacular views but to focus on what God is doing in our midst. And a special problem arises when services are televised and all areas are heavily and indiscriminately lighted. It is possible to work out satisfactory compromises by limiting the areas of high intensity, concealing light fixtures, and designing the controls so the rest of the lighting can function independently when nothing is being televised.

Although the quantity of light in a church interior is an important consideration, even more care is necessary regarding its quality. We seek an ineffability which announces that this is no ordinary space. Both shadows and highlights, colored light and clear light, play their roles. Over the centuries, bright splashes of color on walls and floor have captured the imagination of Christians to make stained glass the most distinctive of religious building materials. And clear light can be just as beautiful when it washes down a textured wall of brick or stone. Light is a most important "building material" in a well-designed church.

It should be recognized that here we are dealing with a highly subjective area. The Christian imagination has been far from consistent in its choices of the quality of light best suited for Christian worship. Some prefer Milton's "dim religious light." It is hard to deny the power of dark shadows, especially overhead, in producing an ineffable quality, hence many churches make an effort to concentrate lighting at pew level so that shadowy recesses abound amid the trusses and rafters overhead. Even with fairly low roofs, this can be accomplished by focusing light directly downward instead of allowing it to diffuse in every direction.

Some think a space is more worshipful when well illuminated, with all areas clearly defined. Many late-Gothic churches were moving toward such a glass-house structure, and churches of the Georgian period were flooded with bright illumination. Light itself is one of the basic symbols of the Christian faith. At the very origins of Gothic, there was a "light mysticism" that reflected on the bright immensities of stained glass, to make the physical building a mirror of the spiritual.

There are no easy answers in this area. Both shadows and highlights reveal the mystery of God, who chooses to dwell among the assembled congregation. Here the sensitivity of an architect is tested as he or she attempts to relate light sources and surfaces to create the best possible environment. The surface treatment of walls, ceilings, and floors will have a major impact on the way light behaves in the interior. Even changing the color of walls a few shades can make a major difference. The architect must view the comprehensive whole to find ways to make the quality of lighting most effective.

Obviously, this is not an area to be entrusted to someone whose occupation is selling light fixtures. Although the quantity of light is important, its quality is even more important, and this involves the ability to conceive of the space as a totality. Most fixtures commercially sold for churches tend to be a kind of ecclesiastical millinery, with the assumption that affixing a cross to a light fixture automatically makes it beautiful and religious. There were no such fixtures until modern times, except for candelabra. When fixtures are necessary today, simple shapes of unobtrusive character are usually preferable. Rheostats are dangerous, since they provide the temptation to make worship a mood-setting affair with a manipulative device, although separate controls for different areas in the church may be desirable. In general, lighting should be constant throughout a service. It is a fine art to keep the quality of lighting as high as possible.

Energy Conservation

Recent years have made churches more sensitive to the need for energy conservation. In some cases this concern has radically altered the design of entire buildings; in most churches it has at least led to the installation of energy-saving devices and equipment. Although energy costs will fluctuate, it is unlikely that we ever again can be as casual about these matters as we often were before the era of cheap energy ended abruptly in the 1970s.

For churches, this is an area not only of architectural responsibility but of moral responsibility as well. One of the norms of church life is that responsibilities always outrun resources. No matter how generous the congregation, there are always obligations of service to the world that cannot be met. Therefore it is immoral to waste money on energy when that money is so greatly needed for the mission of the church. In addition, we now realize that the energy resources of this world are limited, and it is immoral for us to exhaust more than our share. In theological terms, we have moral responsibility for stewardship of both the church's financial resources and the world's natural resources.

These are not always easy decisions, however. Retrofitting an existing building to make it more energy efficient can be costly, and designing a new energy efficient building adds measurably to its cost. However, most of these additional expenses are permanent improvements. Their payout time may be extended, but eventually the cost will be recouped, especially in more severe climates. If the temperature extremes are 40° apart (as in parts of Hawaii), payout for the same work will be slower than in a climate where they are 140° apart (as in Vermont). We have learned that future energy costs are unpredictable, to say the least, but any investment in energy conservation that is likely to be recovered in five or ten years certainly seems morally justifiable if not imperative.

Such expense often includes materials for efficiency of heating, cooling, and lighting. Older stained-glass windows often leak air but frequently merit conservation as works of art. Most churches usually begin with additional glazing and protection in the form of storm windows that can be removed if outdoor temperatures justify opening the windows in summer. Insulation can be installed in walls, ceilings, and under floors if it is absent or deficient. Double sets of entry doors can be added where that is feasible, and all manner of openings can be sealed with caulk, weather stripping, and other devices. Some new churches have been designed so that earthen embankments cover all or parts of the exterior walls. In general, there seems to be a tendency to hug the earth, especially in cold areas.

Other possibilities for energy conservation include more efficient mechanical devices. Older furnaces may give as low as 50 percent efficiency in terms of fuel consumption, whereas newer ones can go as high as 97 percent. Replacement of equipment is never cheap but may pay for itself in time, especially in climates with longer heating or cooling seasons; energy conservation also applies to air conditioning. The most efficient lighting is not always desirable. For example, we would not advise florescent lighting for worship space, although it may be indicated elsewhere in the building, as in Sunday school rooms and work areas.

The increasing cost of energy has become a factor in the growing popularity of a weekday chapel for many congregations. Such a space may be heated comfortably throughout the cold season, whereas the main worship space, little used during the week, may be kept at a much lower temperature, although sufficiently warm to keep pipes from freezing. The chapel requires much less heat, cooling, and light, and may be used for daily services, occasional services such as weddings and funerals, and for private devotions. Groups that might feel intimidated and out of place in the larger Sunday space may feel encouraged to worship in the smaller and more intimate chapel.

Finally, an architect can be expected to be familiar with concerns of energy conservation, and although he or she may need to consult with specialists, advice from someone who can see the total picture is necessary. Otherwise, those who have certain contracting services or equipment to sell will likely find that the church's needs are exactly what they have available. An objective evaluation is necessary to avoid buying goods and services for which there is no real need; that, too, is poor stewardship.

Historic Preservation

Another phenomenon of recent years is the widespread concern with historic preservation. Here also there are moral responsibilities in terms of stewardship, but of a quite different character from those involved in energy conservation. While the latter may call for change, preservation calls for the absence of change. In the case of historic preservation, the moral responsibility will be less in terms of present use and comfort, and more in the direction of obligation to those who preceded us and those who will come after. Anyone who worships in a two-hundred-year-old building realizes that the present generation does not own such a structure, but simply occupies it at one stage in its history. The building may be the chief surviving witness to the faith and worship life of its builders. And that may be a witness that succeeding generations will need to know and appreciate.

Recent years have seen major changes in the worship of most Protestant denominations and among Roman Catholics. In most cases, major architectural alterations have been necessitated. Among Roman Catholics, radical innovations have moved the altar-table away from the wall, simplified its form, and placed the tabernacle elsewhere. All these changes have required difficult decisions, often resulting in compromise between what is necessary to serve the present age and what has served another age well. The question frequently arises: How do we best provide for the worship requirements of today's church without destroying what was equally necessary in the past?

The church is a living organism; it cannot be a museum. Therefore this generation's needs for Christian worship must take precedence. Our attitude throughout this book is that churches are built to be used, not admired: Function is primary, and forms are contingent upon function. The life of the community of faith is our real concern and buildings are there solely to serve that life.

Having said this, several considerations may make us temper our judgment before we rush into a new wave of destroying unwanted images and altar-tables. The events of recent years certainly have taught us that worship can and does change, and with it, the architectural needs of the community. John Ruskin's romantic slogan from 1849, "When we build let us think that we build forever," is no longer valid, if ever it was. Whatever we build must always be somewhat provisional. A new modesty has entered our thinking about church buildings: We recognize that our own requirements do not dictate the needs of succeeding generations, and we should be more reticent about imposing our needs on others. In renovating an existing building, perhaps we should make it possible for others to undo what our times demand so that they can do what their times indicate. We cannot consider our solutions irrevocable, as if they were definitive for Christian worship for all time to come.

Sometimes the answers to our problems may be found in the arrangements of the past. This is especially true in Protestant church buildings built before 1830, but also in much later ones. Frequently the earlier buildings represent a period of worship in which congregational participation was paramount and the people needed to be close to the pulpit and altar-table. Subsequent decades saw a movement toward more monopolizing of the service by the clergy and a tendency for buildings to suggest a holy place remote from the congregation, where clergy and choir alone ventured. Earlier Lord's Tables often were replaced by massive altars fixed against the wall farthest from the congregation. Churches rarely throw anything away, and a careful search may discover the old Lord's Table relegated to a Sunday school room. In some instances, this altar-table has been found superior to the one in current service and has been returned to use. Similar stories could be told about baptismal fonts, and even of pulpits. Quite frequently an earlier arrangement of a building will be found to be more suitable for participatory worship, and the building as a whole, when restored, will have greater integrity. Old photographs may be secured from members and from the local historical society; written documents and records of church repair and improvements can be useful in researching previous arrangements.

Major changes unprecedented in a building's history are frequently necessary to adapt it to contemporary understandings of worship. Before any changes are made, the building should be thoroughly documented for future generations by photographs and written records such as measured drawings. These should be kept in a safe place as part of the congregation's responsibility to those who will inherit the building. (In many cases, this is important even for buildings built in the last twenty years, since the time will come when others will need to know more about post-Vatican II church building.)

When changes are made, it is important to avoid needless destruction. In general, materials identical to those in the original construction should be used. Fiberglass should not take the place of wood when the rest of the structure is wood. The new ingredients should respect the old, even though the previous builders may have been less affluent. In many cases, the old building can be characterized by a single dominant theme in material or decoration, and this theme can be picked up in the new construction.

Quite often it is possible to use some of the best details from an older building for a new purpose. Exquisite pieces may be discovered in some isolated spot and given new prominence. Much modern renovation is in the direction of greater simplification, involving the discarding of an overabundance of images and extra altar-tables. In this process one should watch for hand-carved details that may be used and featured. They will not only provide a link with the building's past but may be of a quality almost impossible to find or to afford today. Certainly much mass-produced merchandise is eminently discardable, but treasures should not be lost.

Major changes often must be made to completely re-orient a building. This demands skillful handling but can be very successful, as exemplified by St. Peter's Roman Catholic Church, Saratoga Springs, New York. There a long tunnel-like nave was changed so that congregational space is wrapped around the altar-table on three sides instead of stretching away from it in one direction. The old chancel became a weekday chapel. Some more timid attempts at renovation have been less successful. When a new altar-table is simply placed in front of the old one, the building proclaims that the "real" altar-table is still in place against the wall; that the new one and what takes place there are purely provisional and temporary. Sometimes portions of an old altar-table can be used in a weekday chapel. Otherwise it is best to have it removed or concealed, along with side altar-tables, so as not to compete for attention with the altar-table actually in use. A weekday chapel may provide the appropriate place to recycle some furnishings.

In many instances, help is available from professionals skilled in historic preservation. Each state now has designated a State Historic Preservation Officer. Hundreds of thousands of buildings have been placed on the National Register of Historic Places as worthy of preservation. The state historic preservation office usually can put one in touch with local professionals who can evaluate the rarity and quality of features in a building. A compromise between preservation and adaptive use may be possible, with results that serve the church well and preserve an important building for the congregation and local area. It is heartbreaking to see beautiful exterior details sacrificed in order to cover a building with vinyl siding. Such vandalism certainly should not occur simply because of ignorance.

Security

Security is a problem most churches face today. While once it was common to leave churches unlocked so that people could enter for prayer and meditation, such practice has become more and more rare. The works of art found in many churches have become a tempting target for thieves; other goods disappear as well when left unprotected. Downtown churches that feel an obligation to remain open may find it necessary to hire security guards, at far too great a cost for most congregations.

One solution is to provide a weekday chapel that can be secured so that entry to the main church is prevented. Such chapels may contain murals or mosaics or other works of art less likely to be subjects of theft. A common sacristy can serve both the chapel and the main church, but it will need to be kept locked to protect church silver and vestments. Such a chapel provides ample opportunity for those who wish to stop by for a moment of prayer, and no one will be offended by locked doors or the presence of a guard.

When new church facilities are being planned, it is frequently possible to situate a reception desk so that one person can survey all the people who enter the building. Such an arrangement makes it easy to help people but discourages those who only want to help themselves to church property.

Since many church meetings are held at night and there is a growing tendency toward more nighttime services such as Christmas Eve, Ash Wednesday, and the Easter Vigil, it is necessary to give serious attention to the exterior lighting of church property. Adequate perimeter lighting around the building, in the parking lots, and on any paths to the building is important for people's safety and will encourage attendance.

Most communities have building codes that include provisions for fire safety — for example, two stairways for balconies. Before any construction is allowed, building permits to ensure conformity with local standards will be necessary. However, the church is responsible not just for minimal code compliance, but for assuring the highest possible degree of safety for all occupants. On occasion, the demands of security and the requirements for fire safety (such as multiple exits) may be in conflict and need to be resolved, but when it comes to safety, the church must place a high value on life and limb, even at extra expense.

Access for Those with Handicaps

The church professes to welcome all people to its services. Yet in many buildings, physical barriers deny them entrance. We have seen a church with twenty-one steps to the interior and no handrail for the top four steps. It is a strange self-contradiction when we invite people and then inhibit their entrance. Certainly these are not intentional contradictions, but they are no less real for the approximately 10 percent of Americans with some disability.

At stake here is a vital issue of justice, the need for the church to affirm the full human worth of all individuals. By denying access to some and restricting degree of participation to others, we essentially deny their full worth. Paul makes it clear that in the church, "God has combined the various parts of the body. . . so that there might be no sense of division in the body, but that all its organs might feel the same concern for one another. If one organ suffers, they all suffer together" (1 Cor. 12:24b-26 NEB). Thus all Christians suffer when any members of the body of Christ are excluded or negated by architectural barriers.

In the middle of the nineteenth century, the advent of the Sunday-school movement necessitated more space for religious instruction. Many churches found the most inexpensive way to provide such space was to place it beneath the worship space, sometimes literally raising the building to add this new area. Only in recent years have we realized the great barrier created by the flight of exterior steps, especially in icy weather. For some people it is tantamount to erecting a "Keep Out" sign.

Secular society has become more conscious of the problems of full accessibility to public places in recent years and, in many cases, has succeeded better than churches. We have learned that these problems are more complex than first realized. A few years ago we were anxious to make curb cuts so wheelchairs were not barred from crossing streets. But now we realize that unless special provisions are made, these sloping curbs are terribly dangerous for blind people, who may walk into a busy intersection without realizing it. Ramps seemed the best way to provide access for wheelchairs until we learned that victims of stroke might be unable to negotiate them. Each year brings discoveries, and each stage of discovery has brought new solutions. Current literature on the subject should be reviewed by congregations that are considering renovation or building.

We can list here only a very few areas that need attention in almost all existing buildings and when planning new ones. The problems presented by stairsteps (either exterior or interior) are obvious. In many climates all exterior entrances can pose difficulties unless they are sheltered. Ramps, steps, or chair lifts should be located inside the building, away from snow and ice. On exterior walkways, avoid overhanging branches or signs.

Inside and out, avoid single steps and mark all changes in ramps, steps, and floor level with colored texture strips. Do not use rugs or mats that may slip; ramps with open sides should have curbs to prevent canes and crutches from slipping. Handrails should extend eighteen inches beyond any landings on stairs and ramps so they can be grasped before entering that level. Railings should have several rows so a child cannot fall through, but vertical supports should be avoided, since they may catch the wheels of a wheelchair.

Doors also pose special problems. For those with arthritic hands, a great deal of door hardware can be cruel, especially if it has sharp edges. Door handles that require twisting or squeezing should be replaced by levers or push plates that allow use of the large muscles or whole body; textured handles help the visually impaired. Glass panels make it possible to see children or wheelchairs on the other side, and metal kickplates allow wheelchairs to open doors; panic-exit bars are a necessary precaution.

Careful planning will ensure that toilet facilities are usable by all. Specially designed equipment is available, but more space is necessary for installation. Cloakroom facilities can be arranged to provide places where people in wheelchairs can hang their coats. In congregational space, areas without pews are appreciated by those in wheelchairs, and a floor that does not slope makes for safer parking. A few pews with extra space between them will benefit those with crutches, canes, or walkers.

In almost any congregation, there will be people with poor hearing or eyesight. Many churches now have copying machines that will double the size of print in the church bulletin at no extra cost, yet few make this effort. Large-print Bibles, hymnals, and service books are available in some instances. Sufficient lighting is necessary also to help those with visual impairments. Those with hearing disabilities will profit from sufficient lighting on those leading the service so that lip-reading is possible; the provision of someone to do signing is even better, and the area in which this person stands also must be well lighted. For those with impaired hearing, special earphones may be made available in designated pews.

Some churches now routinely tape the Sunday service so it can be replayed in sickrooms. With the widespread use of video, it soon may be possible to circulate a videotape of the Sunday service each week to people at home.

All these provisions mean extra expense, but the money is well spent if it makes worship possible for those who otherwise may be prevented. Few churches are completely equipped at present to provide for people with handicapping conditions. And we shall undoubtedly discover other disabilities that have hitherto been neglected. A survey in a major city found that less than one percent of the churches were accessible for wheelchairs. This is reverse evangelism, for it eliminates people rather than attracting them.

There are federal and some state guidelines and legal requirements for accessibility to public spaces. Churches usually are not affected by these but may profit from studying them. Many denominations now publish guidelines for eliminating barriers, and other literature is available.[4]

Liturgical Art

Church architecture provides a setting for all the arts. In recent years the role of visual arts in worship has undergone some major changes. Protestant groups that once feared images of the divine could be idolatrous came to tolerate and eventually welcome them. Roman Catholics, on the other hand, have been repulsed by the surfeit of images in their churches and have removed thousands of plaster saints, sentimental murals, and fake marble altars. Both Protestants and Roman Catholics have come to realize that good liturgical art has an important role in worship and that art of poor quality should be avoided. Art of good quality is important — not because it is pretty but because it helps bring us closer to the object of our worship. In this sense, it is "liturgical" art, not simply "religious" art.

Part of the purpose of liturgical art in the church is to underline the seriousness of what we are about when we gather for worship. This is not a casual assembly; this is the people of God meeting with God. One does not expect fine art in a snack bar but one does expect beautiful surroundings in an elegant restaurant. The Japanese tea ceremony is a good example of the blend of careful ritual and exquisite visual context. Respect for guests in this ceremony is expressed by the care and concern with which all objects involved are selected and handled. The value we place on worship is emphasized by the quality of the environment we provide.

In this sense, there is a radical discontinuity between worship and much of our throw-away culture. What we do when we meet our God has the context of the sublime, and the building and everything in it should proclaim that we are in God's presence. Certainly God has no need of beauty to be present to us, but we often need art to help us remember we are in God's presence. The use of physical objects is one way to perceive spiritual realities. Thus the provision of art in churches is not to delight the eye but to illumine the inner person by suggesting realities that transcend that which is purely physical.

It is good practice to allocate a certain portion of any building or renovating budget for liturgical art. Only a few percentage points set aside for quality art can make a major difference in the total project. In general, it is preferable to secure one excellent object rather than several that are mediocre in quality. We are not recommending a luxury when we advise the purchase of fine art for the church, but emphasizing an important ingredient of the place where humans and God meet.

Frequently the architect will have contacts with artists in the area. Most cities of any size have a college or university nearby, and these almost always have a department of art. Inquiries at museums or galleries in the community often will lead to individuals, either local or elsewhere, who are competent to produce good liturgical art for the church. If these persons are interested, they should talk with the church's representatives to define the community's needs. The church should bear in mind that an artist is a professional and should be paid a commission on the same basis as for secular work.

The competence of an artist is a matter of serious concern, and professional help in evaluating this may be necessary. It is far better to use a secular artist of great talent than one who is pious but whose work is mediocre. Artistic skill and willingness to listen to the religious community are both important. We now realize that even in the catacombs, much of the painting was done by pagan artists who were willing to listen to what the Christian community needed. And some of the best liturgical art of modern times was created by nonbelievers who sought to express the community's beliefs. National competitions of liturgical art and jury selections, sometimes illustrated in *Faith & Form,* can be instructive. In any event, previous works by an artist should be examined before commissioning an original work.

Essentially, liturgical art is art before which we say our prayers. Its chief function is to make visible the unseen presence of God, although the image can never be confused with that which it depicts. It is art that commands us to take off our shoes as we recognize that the ground on which we stand is holy, that we are in the presence of God. No ordinary art will do this. We do not produce a photographic likeness of God, but a representation that points beyond itself to what the inner eye alone can see. Thus there is a transcendent quality to such art. It has power to make present to our minds the transcendent One, just as photographs of loved ones can help to mediate their presence when absent. But unlike the loved one, God is present; we simply need to be reminded of this reality, and liturgical art helps to do this.

A characteristic of liturgical art is its communal character. In a sense, the artist speaks *for* the community rather than to it, aiming not at self-expression but at capturing the essence of that which makes the community one. Each work will bear the imprint of the artist's insight and skill in translating the community's faith into a tangible object. The making of the object is essentially a communal effort, entrusted to one with artistic skill.

We rely heavily on a traditional language of signs and symbols, which have been passed on to us just as the words in which we express our faith have been passed on. The Apostles' and Nicene creeds have served Christians for more than a thousand years. Visual symbols do likewise. We do not ask an artist to develop a whole new iconography; we simply use accepted visual language to express conventional concepts. For example, the cross, the dove, the hand of God—these express a visual tradition shared by the community. This does not mean that the artist is confined to a traditional style. Far from it; having a recognizable vocabulary, he or she can use it in unexperienced ways. It is traditional to be modern, in the sense that each generation needs to say the same thing, but in new ways — ways that make sense in terms of the realities it experiences. So traditional elements may be used in ways and styles previously unknown.

Another characteristic of liturgical art is what we might call its dimension of religious power—its ability to reach a dimension of depth, to push us beyond surface realities. It is the ability, in the centurion's words, to make us say: "Truly this man was the Son of God" (Mark 15:39). Frequently, art that depicts a faithful likeness lacks this dimension; some distortion may say more than a superficial likeness. Thus what the artist is painting, carving, or glazing is really insight — insight which penetrates beneath the surface to the essence of our experience of God.

Much primitive art has this quality; the carved *santos* of New Mexico probably are the most powerful examples of liturgical art produced in this country. In our century, the paintings of Georges Rouault have this dimension of depth. His paintings are not actual depictions of the subject matter but of revelation through that subject. Obviously, such a quality of religious power is difficult to describe. Although it can be experienced, we stretch the limits of spoken language in trying to express it, and perhaps this is exactly why visual art is necessary.

In general, we urge that this art be designed and created in collaboration with the architect. Catalog furnishings and art are necessarily mass-produced. It is generic art, not designed for any specific church, so it may easily clash with the scale and materials of the building. In addition, this "art" frequently costs more than a piece made locally. When poor quality, high cost, and inappropriateness are recognized, one has good reason to avoid art from catalogs. If money is a problem, it is better to commission one good piece and wait until other funds are available for additional works.

We shall mention briefly several of the most common forms of liturgical art. The chief liturgical furnishings— pulpit, altar-table, and baptismal font are objects at the very center of the community's life together and deserve artistic treatment. They should reflect the finest design skills possible and be made of quality materials by highly competent craftspeople. These three objects should be seen as a unit, reflecting similar design features and a common material, especially if they are to be located near one another. The care that goes into providing adequate furnishings is an indication of our belief that God acts in word and sacrament, for which these items are necessary.

Sometimes it is suggested that images, words, or symbols be placed on the pulpit, altar-table, or font, but it should be kept in mind that the form of these items ought

to express their function, and that function is far more eloquent than applied symbols. The pulpit should proclaim
that it is a place for reading; the altar-table, a place for
eating and drinking; and the font, a container for water. It
is the function of the liturgical center that is the essential
symbol, not what is carved or painted upon it, and there is
no need to place a symbol on a symbol. A cross and carved
words do not make an ungainly form a good altar-table,
nor can a legion of painted saints transform a small basin
into an adequate baptismal font.

It may be desirable to place one symbol nearby, such
as a cross or an image, to unite the liturgical center and
give focus to the entire space. A large cross suspended above
the altar-table or on the wall behind it would serve this
purpose well. It should be scaled to the other furnishings
and may be either of similar material or a deliberate contrast. In some cases an image of Christ would fulfill this
function best. If other images are present, they should always be subordinate to the figure of Christ.

We have spoken already about images and symbols,
especially in the form of stained glass, painting, or sculpture. Here one must ask how directly these are related to
the community at worship. Such a piece of art can quickly
become propaganda if it is seen as an object that tells a
story, encourages action, or provokes nostalgia. But if it is
seen as a reminder that the congregation worships "with
Angels and Archangels and with all the company of heaven,"
it can function as liturgical art. In some traditions, carefully worked-out iconographies dictate the proximity of
images of various saints to that of Christ, and the relative
size of each. In every tradition, the Christ figure should
seem to be the most prominent. The purpose of images and
symbols is to make visible Whom we worship, and with
Whom we worship.

Sometimes we are disturbed by abstract art although
we readily accept music, which usually is an abstract art
form. Yet abstract visual art, like music, can speak eloquently about unseen realities, qualities such as awe,

reverence, transcendence, and generosity. Again, we are not talking about decorative art, but art that has a genuine liturgical function in leading us to prayer, and in many cases, abstract use of color and form can do this as well or better than recognizable images and symbols. For some religions, all religious art is abstract.

We have become much more sensitive in recent years to the use of textiles as liturgical art — in vestments, hangings, banners. Textiles can be woven of almost anything that will lie flat (and some things that will not). It is important to recognize the qualities of this medium; too often a textile is required to function as a print medium by the addition of a multitude of words and symbols. Some of the best textile liturgical art says nothing except that this place is important and deserves full attention because something significant happens here. We do not need words to tell us that; we can use color, texture, and form. Fine linen tablecloths do not need words.

Textiles can function in ways no other medium can. Since they are inherently tactile, people tend to examine them by touch. They can humanize wood and stone and brick so that we relate to the objects they cover in a more intimate way. Usually textiles are portable and can be changed as we progress through our yearly recital of the works of Christ. This gives a variety to the building as the feel of the seasons and festivals changes. Something similar happens with flowers — we associate holly with one festival, lilies with another. Change and succession are important in worship. The building should not always remain the same, and textiles can give us a different building for different occasions.

In the case of textiles, basically abstract art forms, the basic form should be allowed to speak. Putting symbols on a stole, for example, is, again, placing a symbol on a symbol. The appliqueing of crosses, triangles, or doves usually detracts from the simple and direct statement made by good texture and appropriate color.

We should allow also for more generous sizes in hangings. Usually one good textile, carefully chosen to reflect the season and occasion, can say more than many small ones. And space must be provided for hanging such textiles in storage when the occasion is past. The variety of textiles we use in worship is enormous: Baptismal robes may clothe tiny babies and funeral palls cover caskets; clerical vestments announce the solemnity and significance of the occasion. Finally, textiles are capable of movement: On a human, textile art moves as an extension of the body; when hangings are placed where air circulates, the textile moves as if it were a live thing.

Books play a very important role in worship, yet we have been slow to recognize this. The way a page is printed may say as much as what is printed on it, yet publishers of hymnals and service books seem more concerned about how much they can cram on a page. If worship is a quality act (the word itself means *ascribing worth*), then objects such as hymnals and service books should show a high standard of design. Page format should be good, typefaces legible and attractive, and paper quality high. Yet most church bulletins and missalettes are the antithesis of all these.

Bookbinding is an important art, yet the modern church rarely takes it seriously. Pulpit Bibles, lectionaries, and Gospel books all play prominent roles in our worship; they should reflect this importance in their quality. Great care should be exercised in choosing commercial editions of these publications. In many cities, skilled bookbinders can create works of art, and they should be employed to bind books of Scripture and service books used at the pulpit, altartable, and font, or those held in the hand, as at weddings. Such important objects must reflect the value we place on what we do in worship. When we read from a paperback Bible, we show we really do not care.

Memorial Gifts

It is a common procedure in many church building or renovation projects to solicit gifts for the construction or for the purchase of various items. This is a dangerous practice, though frequently successful in raising money. First, it puts the church in the position of sales promotion. Since gifts are bought and then donated to the church, people may purchase the most conspicuous items and ignore the less conspicuous, although these may be equally necessary and expensive.

Second, the church may be given items it neither needs nor wants. Yet when someone has given something, it is normal for that person to insist that it be used regularly. Most of the community may have no desire for chimes but when they have been given, the donor is likely to think they must be placed prominently in front of the church and used each Sunday. Such objects often remain long after the donor family has died out or left town. Churches continually find themselves burdened with objects they no longer need.

In every congregation there should be a committee to deal with memorial gifts, and it should have the power and courage to say "No" to unwanted items. It should compile a list of priority items so that when money becomes available these things can be purchased. But care should be exercised that donors are seen as giving money rather than specific items, so that if a congregation changes from one pulpit Bible to another translation, a specific donor is not offended. If certain objects are given despite announced policy, care should be taken that they not be identified with plaques. A memorial book, which may be kept in the narthex, is the best way to record the names of donors.

Certain objects should be avoided. National flags and denominational symbols have no place in Christian worship. We proclaim a universal God, not a local deity. National flags are local and divisive, and originally were banners carried into battle. We sometimes learn that our national agenda may not be the will of God, and flags should be left to various patriotic and military groups. Even denominational flags and symbols are partisan and divisive, not appropriate for the inside of churches; placed outside, they may perform a useful function in identifying the building. The real symbol is the community itself, gathered for worship, and it does not need to be reminded that it is the Roman Catholic, Presbyterian, or United Methodist portion of the Church.

One must, then, look carefully at every gift. Do we really want this object? Do we want to feel obligated to use it? If so, see that it is not ordered from a catalog, but designed by the architect. He or she will know how to make certain the gift relates to the rest of the worship space. Even when the object is made by the person offering the gift, it should be subject to professional scrutiny, with the possibility of polite refusal.

Finally, many objects should be disposed of. One of the biggest obstacles to renovation is what is already in place. Many churches have solved this problem by building a memorial room or hallway in which gifts the church has outgrown can be preserved. Most families have a drawer or closet for objects that once were used and treasured but now are outgrown. Still, they can grace the walls of a room or corridor. Old stained glass inappropriate for a new building can create considerable interest when it lines a corridor. Thus the old gives way to new — perhaps not to something better, but to something more appropriate for Christian worship as we know it in our time and place.

Ten

RESOURCES

I. Denominational Resources

Any congregation planning to build or renovate should immediately contact denominational authorities for any publications, consulting services, and procedural advice they have to offer. In some instances, help is available on the regional level (diocesan, presbytery, conference, etc.); in others, it will involve national staff in the areas of worship, church extension, homeland ministries, or national missions. Frequently there are publications that explain denominational procedure and indicate roles and responsibilities within and beyond the congregation; there may be free or low-cost publications or other visual materials. These sources of information generally will be current and certainly ought to be consulted and heeded.

II. Periodicals

Only three current periodicals in English deal exclusively with church architecture:

Cutting Edge: Published quarterly by the Board of Church Extension of Disciples of Christ, P.O. Box 7030, Indianapolis, IN 46207. This consists of a series of articles on various aspects of "planning and financing physical facilities for congregations and units of the Christian Church (Disciples of Christ)." Members of other denominations will find the articles useful.

Faith & Form. Published semiannually by the Interfaith Forum on Religion, Art, and Architecture, 1777 Church St. NW, Washington, DC 20036. This remains the most current source of information, with excellent articles and photographs of church buildings and liturgical art. Buildings and objects receiving awards in national competitions are often illustrated; recent books on church architecture are reviewed.

Art & Environment Newsletter (Chicago: Liturgy Training Publications, 1800 North Hermitage Avenue, Chicago, IL 60622-1101) A Roman Catholic periodical, often useful to others.

See Also:

Liturgical Arts Quarterly. From 1931 until 1972 this was the world's leading periodical on this subject. Many articles and photographs dealing with architecture are still of value.

III. Books

Listed here are select books of interest to those responsible for church building today. This list does not include books that are primarily collections of photographs of contemporary buildings or those that are entirely historical in scope. The brief comments here are intended only to point out the distinctive features of each book. Books in print as of 1998 are marked by an asterisk; others may be found in libraries. All are chosen to reflect architectural solutions to changes in worship in the last twenty-five years.

*Bishops' Committee on the Liturgy. *Environment and Art in Catholic Worship.* Washington: United States Catholic Conference Publications Office (1312 Massachusetts Ave. NW, Washington, DC 20005), 1978. Despite the title, everyone concerned with church architecture should read the text and examine the plates with care. A more recent edition (1986) with different illustrations can be ordered from Liturgy Training Publications, 1800 N. Hermitage Ave., Chicago, IL 60622-1101.

Brown, Bill, ed. *Building and Renovation Kit for Places of Catholic Worship.* Chicago: Liturgy Training Publications, 1982. This is the most complete of the various diocesan publications for building committees. Includes books on introduction, process, tools, resources, guidelines. Other resources have been put out by such dioceses as Portland, Maine (1965), Albany (1970), Louisville (1977), Seattle (1981), Green Bay (1982), Brooklyn (n.d.), Cincinnati (n.d.), and Buffalo (1986).

Bruggink, Donald J., and Droppers, Carl H. *Christ and Architecture: Building Presbyterian/Reformed Churches.* Grand Rapids: Eerdmans Publishing Co., 1965. A definitive study based on careful historical and theological study of building for Reformed worship. Written by a theologian and an architect. Well illustrated.

_____. *When Faith Takes Form.* Grand Rapids: Eerdmans Publishing Co., 1971. Principles of church architecture illustrated in a number of outstanding recent buildings. The reader eavesdrops on conversations between a theologian and an architect regarding each building.

Cope, Gilbert, ed. *Making the Building Serve the Liturgy: Studies in the Re-ordering of Churches.* London: A. R. Mowbray & Co., 1962. A series of essays discussing rearrangements necessary to make Anglican churches suitable for the changing practices in worship.

Dahinden, Justus. *New Trends in Church Architecture.* New York: Universe Books, 1967. A distinguished Swiss architect writes about recent developments, illustrating his points with new churches in Europe and Africa.

Davies, J. G. *The Architectural Setting of Baptism.* London: Barrie & Rockliff, 1962. A historical study of fonts, baptismal pools, and their settings. Helpful in making current decisions on the basis of the problems and solutions that developed over the centuries.

Debuyst, Frederic. *Modern Architecture and Christian Celebration.* Richmond: John Knox Press, 1968. A brief classic statement of the goals of post-Vatican II architecture by a Belgian monk.

Hammond, Peter. *Liturgy and Architecture.* New York: Columbia University Press, 1961. A pioneering book describes the developments in liturgical architecture prior to Vatican II and indicates many of the trends that were to follow.

_____, ed. *Towards a Church Architecture.* London: Architectural Press, 1962. A series of serious essays outlining the shape of reforms about to occur in the following two decades.

Hayes, Bartlett. *Tradition Becomes Innovation: Modern Religious Architecture in America.* New York: Pilgrim Press, 1983. The most recent illustrated survey of new church building and liturgical art in America. Includes good examples from all religious traditions.

Hickman, Hoyt L. *A Primer for Church Worship.* Nashville: Abingdon Press, 1984. A simple introductory study of Christian worship, written for a lay audience. A good beginning point for congregational study.

Lockett, William, ed. *The Modern Architectural Setting of the Liturgy.* London: S.P.C.K., 1964. A collection of essays from a variety of traditions concerned with the expression of modern worship needs in architectural terms.

Lynn, Edwin C. *Tired Dragons: Adapting Church Architecture to Changing Needs.* Boston: Beacon Press, 1972.

Encompasses every aspect of the church building, by a Protestant minister who is also an architect; deals in a comprehensive way with the problems encountered in rejuvenating older buildings.

Meeting House Essays (Chicago: Liturgy Training Publications, 1990-1996).
    I. Laurence A. Hoffman. *Sacred Places and the Pilgrimage of Life*
    II. *Acoustics for Liturgy*
    III. Peter E. Smith. *Cherubim of Gold: Building Materials and Aesthetics*
    IV. John Buscemi. *Places for Devotion*
    V. Michael E. DeSanctis. *Renewing the City of God: The Reform of Catholic Architecture in the United States.*
    VI. Michael Jones-Frank. *Iconography and Liturgy*
    VII. Viggo Bech Rambusch. *Lighting the Liturgy.*
    VIII. Richard S. Vosko. *Designing Future Worship Spaces.*
A series of small books on topics relevant to most Christians.

New Churches Research Group. *Church Buildings: A Guide to Planning and Design.* London: Architects' Journal Information Library, 1967. A series of articles giving design requirements and measurements for worship in the principal religious bodies in England.

Sövik, Edward A. *Architecture for Worship.* Minneapolis: Augsburg Publishing House, 1973. An excellent general treatment by a distinguished architect with a clear preference for flexible church space (a centrum) and gathering space (a concourse).

United States Catholic Conference. *The Environment for Worship: A Reader.* Washington: United States Catholic Conference Publications Office, 1980. A collection of excellent articles dealing with basic considerations for church building and renovation.

Vosko, Richard. *Through the Eye of a Rose Window: A Perspective on the Environment for Worship.* Saratoga, Calif.: Resource Publications, 1981. A recent review of requirements for Roman Catholic worship, expressed in concise and readable form by a priest who is an interior designer and educator.

*White, James F. *Introduction to Christian Worship.* Revised Edition. Nashville: Abingdon Press, 1990. A general introduction to Christian worship as practiced in the major western churches; deals with basic concerns of the subject historically, theologically, and practically, in a comprehensive fashion. Provides much background material.

*_____. *Christian Worship in North America, A Retrospective:1955-1995.* Collegeville: Liturgical Press, 1997. This includes several articles on church architecture, especially several on the history of Protestant building for worship.

*White, Susan J. *Art, Architecture, and Liturgical Reform.* New York: Pueblo, 1990. A study of the impact of the liturgical movement on the shape of the environment for Christian worship.

*_____. *Groundwork of Christian Worship.* London: Epworth Press, 1997. A basic introduction to the problems and possibilities of Christian worship, in an attempt to answer the question: "Why do Christians worship as they do?" Provides case studies for congregational reflection.

NOTES

1. *An Apology for the True Christian Divinity* (Manchester: William Irvin, 1869), p. 240

2. Edward Sövik, *Architecture for Worship* (Minneapolis: Augsburg Press, 1973), p. 71

3. For a detailed description of this historic development, see James F. White, *Protestant Worship and Church Architecture* (New York: Oxford University Press, 1964), chaps. 4,5. For a shorter account, see White, *Introduction to Christian Worship,* Revised Edition (Nashville: Abingdon Press, 1990), chap. 3

4. Edward Sövik's *Accessible Church Buildings* (New York: Pilgrim Press, 1981) is out of print, but may be found in libraries or possibly purchased from Pilgrim Press, 132 W. 31st St., New York, NY 10001. An article by Jerry Ellis, "Architectural Barriers," in *Study and Plans Committee Workbook,* is available from the Board of Church Extension, Disciples of Christ, P.O. Box 7030, Indianapolis, IN 46207

INDEX